9 + 9 EQUALS 9

THE EQUATION OF LIFE'S TRANSITIONS

ANTHONY L. SCOTT

We want to hear from you. Please share your comments through any of the communication methods provided below. Thank you.

---

9 + 9

EQUALS 9

THE EQUATION OF LIFE'S TRANSITIONS

E-mail: ascott@cite2020.com
Facebook: facebook.com/ cite2020
Twitter: @cite2020

ISBN-13: 9781482733488
ISBN-10: 148273348X

Library of Congress Control Number: 2013907661
Printed in the United States of America

Cover Design by:
Bryan Wilson - Amalgam Creative Solutions

DEDICATION

To my Creator God, Lord and Savior Jesus Christ, and Helper Holy Spirit:

I recognize You as the source of my life, and realize that apart from You, I can do nothing but through You, I can do all things. Thank You for Your unfailing love that has always given me strength.

I love You.

To my biggest fan and strongest support, my wife, Melanie:

Since the days we academically competed with each other in college, you have always encouraged the leader within me to arise. Through every ebb and flow of our relationship, your love and protection of me are always constants and can never be questioned. Thank you for all you have personally delayed that the dreams in me would be realized. I sure am grateful to have you by my side.

I love you.

To four amazing sons who have captivated my heart—AJ, Christian, Jason, and Justin:

Thank you for the priceless opportunity of being your father and for instilling a joy in me that rests in the reality that what I have begun, you will further build and perpetuate beyond my lifetime.

Daddy loves you.

TABLE OF CONTENTS

ACKNOWLEDGMENTS

It takes a village to raise a child. I think almost everyone has heard this common phrase uttered at least once in his or her lifetime. In many regards, this statement is true.

I can name several individuals who contributed to the person I am and am daily becoming. On that note, I would like to acknowledge my parents, Arthur and Ida Scott, for providing the love and resources I needed to chart a successful and significant life; my brother, Gene Scott, for teaching me even when you weren't saying anything; my maternal grandparents, Nelson and Ida Mae Petree, for your demonstration of faith and having a home that served as a safe place; and my paternal grandparents, Arthur and Lillie Scott, for being a reminder of the strength experienced through family and community. I also would like to thank a special cousin, Nel Quash, who was likened to a second mother to me, and my in-laws, Jimmy and Corlis Ellis, for welcoming me into your family, and most important, for bringing my wife into the world (smile). I thank my friend and mentor, Randall Worley, for our "coincidence"; my good friend, Donna Bouie, for your timely wisdom and encouragement; the many uncles, aunts, and cousins it would take a family tree to list; all friends who have encouraged and assisted me in this work as well as supported me during varying dispensations of my life (you know who you are); my marketing team, Lanaire Lindo and Angette Williams, for your time and insight; my graphic designer, Bryan Wilson, for capturing the concept for this book's cover (the design is a reflection of the book's message); and my CreateSpace project team, for providing quality editorial and interior design services. To all mentioned, and my other family and friends in those who read this book, I say:

FULL LIFE AHEAD...
FOCUS ONLY ON THAT WHICH MATTERS MOST!

—Anthony L. Scott

A MESSAGE FROM THE AUTHOR'S WIFE

My grandparents taught me how to be a straight shooter. I was taught to be 100% honest and add no fluff, and this is what I observed growing up. Now don't get me wrong, there was no lack of affection, hugs and kisses, and mushy stuff. But when it came to fundamentals, lessons to be learned, and development, it was serious business.

Let me personally tell you that my husband views your life and legacy as serious business. Who you are and who you are to become matters to him. The peace and joy that we experience are what he desires for every person who picks up this book. There is no room to be mushy in the transitions of your life because you matter. Your life is of great significance!

His genuine interest of others can often be seen when Anthony teaches. He has a reputation for using visual aids to enhance the points he wants to ensure are clearly understood. Even young children remember "Mr. Anthony" holding up the truck with multiple cars when he taught on the power of unity and collaboration. There are some who still remember the principles articulated when he used a t-shirt to talk about personal branding and strategic marketing, a name badge to express how God has a unique relationship with each of us, and a plumb line to reflect God's desire to bring us into alignment with His will. As a result of these and other teaching materials, my husband has often been called "Mr. VA", standing for "Mr. Visual Aid." This book presents yet another visual aid from Mr. VA's playbook. This time, instead of a truck, t-shirt, name badge, or plumb line, Anthony *is* the visual aid. His life events, pain, decisions, and rewards are on display for you to get the message God wants to deliver to you.

A graduation. An aspiring career out of college. An engagement. A wedding. New relationships. Two children. A layoff after nine years. A miscarriage. A third child. Another miscarriage. Broken relationships. A fourth child. New life! That's a summary of the last thirteen years of my life to paint the picture that our lives are made up of countless transitions. How many we experience is of no value when compared to how we steward them. If a team doesn't execute the right plays and strategies, their chance of winning a game is much less. If you don't make the right transitions in your life, your opportunity to fulfill destiny and experience abundant living will be met with greater resistance. I don't know where you are, but I do know this—regardless of where you are, 9 + 9 EQUALS 9 is guaranteed to help you thrive and have the proper perspective in any transition. I didn't have this resource when I needed it during the last thirteen years, but now that I do, I am more equipped to master the art of transition. I know you will too as you explore the 9 + 9 EQUALS 9 journey.

9 + 9 EQUALS 9 is an effective guide to helping you not only see the transitions in your life you need to make, but also provide you the wisdom and confidence to follow through and live after the transitions. In this personal work, my husband will share with you one of the most difficult transitions he ever made. I was right there with him during this time of hurt and pain that was soon followed by invaluable peace and joy. I am a witness that everything shared in this book is true and from his heart. Although the boys and I were silent riders on this journey with my husband, we had a great deal to lose if Anthony forfeited the transition shared with you in the coming pages. To my husband, I say *Bravo!* Here is your standing ovation for saving your legacy and being a man after God's own heart.

—*Melanie E. Scott*

FOREWORD

BY

DR. RANDALL WORLEY

I am in transition. Translation: *I am not where I was, and not yet where I am going.* Transition is the undefinable, mysterious space between where you've been, and who you are becoming. It is that uneasy feeling of being in between. One foot on the dock, the other in the boat. One foot is on something stationary, the other on something buoyant that is leaving with or without you. From birth to burial, life is comprised of transitions. You are either entering one, in one, or leaving one to enter another.

The lessons of life are not learned in a course, but on a course. Transitions are not electives, but vital parts of life's curriculum. It has been said that "growing things change, changing things grow, and changing things challenge us." In the information age, many mistakenly believe that information alone results in transformation. However, transition occurs when we successfully translate what is changing in us, in relationship to what is changing around us. What happens in you while you wait, is as important as what you are waiting for. As the proverb states, "When the student is ready, the teacher will appear."

Jesus said that "as many as received Him, He gave the power to become the sons of God" (John 1:12 KJV). Our new birth is only a beginning, with a view to a life process of becoming. We don't live to eventually experience eternal life after we die. In other words, we don't live *for* eternal life, but *from* eternal life. Eternal life does not describe the length of one's existence, but the quality of it. God has given you the power to become, to evolve. Life is not just about where you came from, but who you are becoming between birth and burial. Many people know when they were born, where they were born, and to whom they were born, but not *why* they were born. Transitions are the reminders of how truth transforms you, and why you manifested in time.

From the moment God sent this planet spinning in its orbit, it has been governed by seasons. Our calendar marks the first day of winter, spring, summer, and fall, but we all know the climate does not always get the memo. After a long bitter winter, the calendar may say that spring has sprung, but the temperature contradicts how things should be. The interim can seem interminable. We look forward to a day when a seamless transition will take place, but instead we find ourselves muttering "how much longer" or "I should have been there by now." Then, one morning, you walk out the door to start your day and something happened over night, or so it seems. Before you ever get to your car, you shed your winter coat. Instead of turning up the heat, you turn on the A/C. By the end of the day, you know it is time for a change of wardrobe.

Solomon said, "to everything there is a season, a time for every purpose under heaven" (Ecclesiastes 3:1). In this very personal work, Anthony Scott allows you to look into a season in his life when he realized the climate had changed, and he had to make a wardrobe change for the new season. Most books on this subject set forth sterile principles, but Anthony Scott, through transparency and vulnerability, has given pulse to the principles. The word becomes flesh, as he explains the *how* that leads to the *where*. As you read about the ebb and flow of his journey, you will be given the confidence to take the step from the known to the glorious unknown, as grace fills the vacuum to reintroduce you.

—Dr. Randall Worley
www.randallworley.com

Every new beginning comes from
some other beginning's end.
—*Seneca*

The secret of change is to focus all of your energy, not on
fighting the old, but building the new.
—*Socrates*

PREFACE

Welcome to the story of *our* lives! My heart is filled with great excitement in hope that this book will encourage you to identify the patterns of your life as you seek complete fulfillment of your purpose and destiny.

From the moment we enter into this world through the birth canal, life is filled with *transitions*. Some are imposed on us naturally. Some we choose. Some we avoid, mainly because of our tendency to hold on to what has become familiar to us. I wrote this book during one of the most transitional periods of my life, which likely poses true for most authors. I will not get into much of my story this early, but I am certain that as you read the last sentence of the last chapter, you will know more about me. However, given I don't desire to dive into the pool of narcissism, it is my heartfelt desire that you will know more about you and how the jigsaw of your life connects to reveal an amazing image. The greatest joy I would have is in knowing that the few words within the pages of this book have recharged someone's battery to live again as they have embraced the understanding of the cycles and patterns of life that every human soul must experience.

This work is not meant to woo the reader with some deep knowledge I have researched and studied for years. I am a husband and father of four sons (all of whom are presently under the age of ten). In other words, between business and family priorities, I don't have much time to spend in research. What I have, I give to you, and that is my life, which is the greatest treasure one can ever offer to another.

So again, welcome to *our* story! I look forward to you getting to know me, as I have already peeked a great deal into your life and know more about you than you think.

CHAPTER 1

NOT 18

You must look within for value
but must look beyond for perspective.
—Denis Waitley

Surely as you read the title of this book, your mind (at least the part of it that likes mathematics) may have subconsciously denied that 9 + 9 = 9. That's fair. I often do flashcards with my two oldest sons, AJ and Christian, and I am sure that if I presented them with the equation 9 + 9, they would immediately shout, "Eighteen!", and give me a high-five in the excitement of returning an answer that they know to be correct. Can't we all relate to the exhilarating feeling of self-confidence when we know something of truth that cannot be debated? Who is going to spend their time telling you that 9 + 9 does not equal eighteen? Not many people, unless they have dared to redefine the arithmetic system. Simply put, 9 + 9 = 18.

Now look at what I have named this chapter: "*NOT 18.*" You are probably wondering why I have titled this work *9 + 9 EQUALS 9*, and initiated it with a chapter labeled "*NOT 18.*" Am I crazy? Am I the individual I speak about in the first paragraph, who, within a split second, has dared to defy what has been taught as a truth in the world of arithmetic? Am I trying to get into a debate with my oldest son, AJ, who happens to be the youngest lawyer I know? Am I trying to bring utter confusion to you to provoke you to put this book down and wonder why you even invested your money in it? Or quite possibly, did I pique your interest and curiosity, which will entice your eyes to continue reading?

I hope that the latter is true—that you are intrigued to know where I am going with this. Trust me and at least get through the first chapter before you infer that I am insane. Actually, I am *in-sane;* I find myself *in* a realm of *sanity* because I have discovered some commonalities across all individuals. I don't want to speak for you, but I find that the greatest literary pieces I have read are those in which I can find myself in the author's imagery. My passion to complete reading a book escalates when I can quickly connect how it relates to me regarding my journey in life. It may relate to me through family, finances, business, relationships, faith, struggles, or a host of other things. The point is that we naturally have an affinity to what best aligns to our life's experiences. So if you saw me reading a book about being single, well, then, maybe you can truly label me as insane (especially if I am reading it in front of my wife). The greatest encouragement comes from those who can clearly relate to a path your life has taken. It brings hope to know that others have ventured down similar roads, confirming you are not alone. Even more, it expresses the power and strength in how one sharing his or her story imparts life into someone reading it. I will share more about this later on as I draw parallels from some of the resources that have granted me understanding.

The title of the book may intrigue you, and while it is about my life, it applies to every person who has been born. That's right. These writings connect with every human soul that has *transitioned* from being a thought in the mind of God to having a human experience on the earth. You think it's a bold (not to be taken as arrogant) statement to say my life parallels that of all persons, huh? Bold as it may sound, it is my humble belief that what you read in the subsequent pages will cause you to reflect on your own experiences and *transitions*. Every person's life has uniqueness and travels altering paths, but some absolutes apply to all individuals, regardless of ethnicity, nation, country, age, social class, and so forth. These are common denominators in life that keep us all connected. For one thing, you, I, and every person who has entered this world had to come through the womb of a mother (we will reference this a little later). Every person who has graced this dimension we call earth has

Every person's life has uniqueness and travels altering paths, but some absolutes apply to all individuals, regardless of ethnicity, nation, country, age, social class, and so forth.

encountered a 9 + 9 moment, and actually, several of them. Don't ponder what this all means now. With the turn of every page in this book, your understanding will increase. But first, let me get back to the title of this chapter: *"NOT 18."*

All you teachers, math majors, scholars, professors, and the like, with all of my southern kindness, I am going to ask you to turn off your mathematics mode. Walk through this book with a perspective that, for the purposes of unlocking potential, giving understanding, destroying fear, providing the tools to liberate invaluable lives from relationships, systems, behaviors, and attitudes of bondage and captivity, igniting dreams, restoring hope, and pursuing destiny, 9 + 9 is ***not*** eighteen. In fact, you will probably shake your head even more when I tell you 9 + 9 equates a value higher than eighteen. No, not nineteen, twenty…continue reading and this will soon become much clearer.

CHAPTER 2

WHAT'S IN A NUMBER?

The numbers don't lie.
—POPULAR SAYING

Just the other day, I went to my physician for my annual physical. As is customary for my routine checkups, the nurse took my blood pressure and had me step on a scale for my weight. Blood pressure was normal, as expected, but what I didn't expect was the numeric value the scale returned as my weight. I didn't feel I had gained any weight, so could the scale be defective? As my wife would say, "Absolutely not." At the conclusion of my physical, I had a conversation with my doctor regarding my health. He said I was doing well but per the *numbers*, he would recommend I try to reduce my weight by ten pounds. In that moment, I recognized I would need to bring some discipline to my eating *choices*, and I was reminded that, while I didn't think I had gained any weight, *the numbers didn't lie*.

I am sure you can somehow relate to this story, whether it is your weight, age, finances, etc. You might think you are twenty-one, but what does the birth certificate reveal?

You might think you have more in your account, but what does that bank statement say? Sure, faith is great, but faith doesn't negate the facts—*the numbers don't lie.*

Numbers are revelatory by nature: they tell us things we may or may not want to accept. In the last chapter, I stated that 9 + 9 is *not* eighteen (not mathematically), and now this chapter has me posing the question, *"what's in a number?"*

One, two, three, four, five, six, seven, eight, nine…how many times have you referenced numbers in the course of a day and pondered whether numbers could actually mean more than their narrowed focus of mathematics? Have you ever looked at significant milestones in your life and the dates on which they occurred and thought there might be some underlying symbolism as to *when* something actually happened? Well, if you haven't, you should start because numbers reveal much more about your life than you may have ascribed. Let me give you an example.

Numbers are revelatory by nature: they tell us things we may or may not want to accept.

My youngest son's name is Justin. In conducting some research on this name, you will find it means justice, order, alignment, and sequence. Justin was born on October 11, 2012. In other words, he was born on 10-11-12. My son, whose name means order, alignment, and sequence, was born on the *only* day in 2012 where the numbers fell in sequence—ten, eleven, twelve. He did not have to be induced, as it was God's plan for him to come on this special day, which has given his mother and me some insight about who this little boy will become—a person who will have the ability to enact peace, righteousness, and justice in situations of disorder. In essence, if you find yourself dealing with a lot of chaos and confusion, start hanging out with Justin and watch your life take a chiropractic adjustment because of his innate nature.

Justin's birthdate shows that numbers can point to a broader reality. The focus of this book is not to provide a deep, analytical breakdown of the numbers game. Internet articles and other books can provide that. If you end this book more focused on a number than the true examination of your life, you have missed beholding the treasure, and I have not achieved my goal. So I kindly ask you to remove all limits and broaden your view because *introspection* is ready to meet you.

Even how this book began supports the idea of how numbers reveal a broader reality. On Sunday, September 9, 2012, I arose from my bed at 3:00 a.m. EST after a few hours of good sleep (this doesn't mean I was snoring). As was my custom every night, I visited the rooms of my sons to check the temperature and ensure they were sleeping well. Due to a commitment I had for later Sunday morning, I knew I would need to get back to sleep right away to catch more rest before my next rising. However, as I am sure you have often experienced, at times it is not that easy to go back to sleep. Well, (fortunately) this was one of those times for me.

I parked myself back into my comfortable sheets, and through a focused closing of the eyelids, made a sincere attempt to rediscover my state of slumber. Turn after turn, position after position, it became evident to me that I was probably not going back to sleep any time soon. So what was a guy to do? Pull out my Smartphone and play a game; go downstairs to my office and read; post a message via social media; grasp the remote in anticipation that some good programming would be on, not just infomercials; get back up and go exercise (OK, this didn't even cross my mind once although I needed to lose ten pounds); or simply lie there, giving my mind a time to consider and reflect. Many times, the TV would have prevailed, and I am sure it has for you too, so don't hold me in contempt. But in this unique moment, the internal desire within me was simply to be still and know that I was *awakened* in this hour for a reason beyond that of checking on my sons.

As I lay there, patiently, awaiting the pit stops my mind would take, I immediately came to a juncture whereby I pulled out my phone to check the date. As I saw the date 09.09.12 illuminate the darkness, it was as if my mind took a quantum leap that I later came to associate with a quick reflection on the previous years of my life, knowing that in just three days I would be celebrating another birthday (09.12.12). At this intense moment where I am sure the chemical processes in my brain looked like the artwork of my two-year-old son (scribble scrabble), I began to lock in on this day and could not go back to sleep. At this point, this book was inspired, on the day of 09-09, later defining this work as *9 + 9 EQUALS 9.*

So *what's in a number*? Much more than what we can quantify because our lives are comprised of innumerable *transitions*. The treasure is in knowing that a number is symbolic to a greater picture. Let me encourage you to closely examine how numbers may connect to the patterns of your life. Allow this book to be a catalyst to get you started. And since Nine is my fellow character in this story, let's give him the opportunity to shed some light on a few things so that we can grow in our understanding together.

"Number Nine, please introduce yourself."

CHAPTER 3

I AM NINE

Without knowing what I am and why I am here,
life is impossible.
—*Leo Tolstoy*

Welcome, my distinguished friends. It is so good to meet you. I am Nine, and I am so privileged and honored to be the one chosen to share with you. In my simplest form, I am aware that you already know me. I am the one who comes after eight and before ten. However, has it ever dawned on you that you don't know everything about me? Let me tell you a little bit about myself.

- I am the highest single-digit number in the decimal system.[1]
  - 1, 2, 3, 4, 5, 6, 7, 8, **9**, 10
- If you multiply me by any natural number and repeatedly add the digits to the answer until it is just one digit, you will end up with me.[1]

[1] "9 (number)," *Wikipedia*, last modified May 22, 2013, accessed May 2013, https://en.wikipedia.org/wiki/9_(number).

    - 2 x **9** = 18 (1 + 8 = **9**)
    - 3 x **9** = 27 (2 + 7 = **9**)
    - 234 x **9** = 2106 (2 + 1 + 0 + 6 = **9**)

- In chemistry, I represent the purity of chemicals.[1]
    - **Nines** are an informal yet common method of grading the purity of very fine precious metals such as platinum, gold, and silver.
- I am the expected full term for a human pregnancy.[1]
    - The **ninth** month of a woman's pregnancy concludes the final trimester.

Here are some common idioms and themes that you may be familiar with:

- A cat-o'-**nine** tails suggests perfect punishment and atonement. It is called this because it is typically made up of **nine** knotted thongs of cotton cord designed to lacerate the skin and cause intense pain.[1] *[Mental Note: Pain is often a part of a major transition.]*
- A police dog, often referred to as a K**9** in some areas, is a dog trained specifically to assist police and other law enforcement personnel in their work.[1]
- Someone dressed to the **nines** is dressed up in fine attire.[1]
- "**Nine** to five" is an expression in the United States originating from the traditional American business hours of 9:00 a.m. to 5:00 p.m., Monday through Friday,

representing a workweek of five eight-hour days comprising forty hours in total.[2]

- "Cloud **nine**" or "on cloud **nine**" refers to a state of elation or happiness, feeling like you are floating on air.[1] *[Mental Note: Joy and peace are the end results after making the right transition.]*

I could share a little more, but as the author stated earlier, the goal is to not woo you with in-depth knowledge and analysis. You get the point that there's more to numbers than what you may have learned. As you read this work, you will find how my DNA and associations mentioned above parallel to your life. You will still not know everything about me, just as I couldn't possibly know everything about you in the short time we have together. I would have to examine your character, life, and actions more closely to *know* you. In fact, I think you will find I have been doing this and *know* you much better than you think.

As the author previously stated, the focus is not about me or any other number. It's merely to connect the dots of your life to symbols and patterns that reveal something greater. Any of my friends—one, three, five, seven, eight, etc.— could tell you that if you seek, you will find. The author has sought more about me, and as a result, has found astonishing parallels to his own life. He and I have gotten to know each other extremely well. We've become

---

[2] "9 (number)," *Wikipedia*, last modified May 22, 2013, accessed May 2013, https://en.wikipedia.org/wiki/9_(number).

the best of friends. In the next chapter, we will narrate together to most effectively reveal the value of examining every intricate part of your life and finding meaning in it.

"Author, can you move us forward?"

CHAPTER 4

THE FIRST ADDEND: THE LEADING NINE

(9 + 9 EQUALS 9)

↑

The First Addend: The Leading Nine

The tomorrow that you desire and envision may never come to pass if you do not end some things you are doing today.
—Dr. Henry Cloud

"Ten-four. Copy that, Nine."

Friends, I hope you are more acquainted with Nine after his pleasant introduction. In mathematics, the *addend* is any one of two or more numbers added together to form a sum.[1] You mathematically astute individuals may have already known this, but a refresher never hurts anyone. For example, if an equation is 5 + 7 = 12, the five and seven are both considered *addends*. Based on this definition, the nines on either side of the plus symbol (9 + 9) are *addends*.

[1] *Dictionary.com*, "Addend," accessed May 2013, http://dictionary.reference.com/browse/addend?s=t.

This chapter aims to focus on the first nine, thus the title, *"The First Addend: The Leading Nine."*

In my day-to-day responsibilities, I play many different roles. I am husband to my wife, father to my children, son to my parents, employee to my employer, consultant to my clients, team player to my colleagues, friend to my friends, and mentor to my mentees. My character and inner being strive to be consistent across all roles while each role is vastly distinct from the others.

Why am I saying this? Because Nine carries with him various meanings and connotations, two of which we are going to explore. Nine is not double-minded or two-faced. His very nature is constant, yet flexibility and versatility are his strengths. Nine may present one aspect to me today, while presenting a very different aspect to one of my friends at the very same time. It's kind of like Nine meets each individual where he or she is in life's journey. Let me bring you closer into my life to show you how.

Nine years (2003) to the time I began to pen this work (September 9, 2012), my life encompassed two significant moments. The first was my opportunity to be an active leader and contributor of a ministry (hereafter referred to as nonprofit). After months of searching, I became ecstatic at the possibility of serving the community and greater Charlotte, North Carolina, area through an organization I believed carried a great mission that aligned to my personal values. Second, my wife became pregnant with our first son in this very same year. What astounding joy, evident by the tears in our eyes as we watched a pregnancy test reveal positive. Just a little more than a year into marriage, we quickly found ourselves preparing to be parents. What a turn of events! My wife and I even experienced our first ever (definitely not our last) cruise in 2003. Let's just say 2003 was a year of firsts in my life that can never be erased or forgotten. It marked a time of *new beginnings*.

Now let's fast forward to 2012. As with 2003, 2012 was a pivotal stage in my life. In the early part of 2012, my leadership and contribution to the nonprofit organization I partnered with in 2003 came to an *abrupt (unplanned)* end. What began as a volunteer/servant leader role evolved into an executive/staff role in 2006. This required more of my time, effort, and concentration to strengthening the vision of the organization and its stakeholders. Nine (9) years later, I found myself *transitioning* from the volunteer and executive leadership roles to a land of uncertainty, the abyss of the unknown because my decision led me to a place I had *never* been before, the place of not knowing my next means of employment (financial compensation).

When I was a junior in college, I landed an internship before my senior year. When I graduated college, I started my professional career with a leading consulting firm. When I departed from that company, I carried my consulting expertise into the nonprofit arena. When I decided to exit my employment from the nonprofit, no doorway was *visibly* open waiting for me to walk through it. Here I was, not having done a résumé in twelve years, mentally regrouping in a time of desperation. You may be asking why I would conclude my employment with nothing else lined up. You will soon find out.

Without an invitation, stress and intense pressure visited me as I *transitioned* from a consistent direct deposit every two weeks to wondering if I could further advance my career in such an unstable economic climate (the US economy and job market still had not fully recovered from the 2008 downturn). It became one of my greatest tests in life. How would I face adversity when market conditions were volatile, my wife was no longer employed, I had three children in my home and one more on the way, a mortgage with relative expenses to manage a home, and financial debt? This doesn't sound too uncommon, given the number of Americans that have been in similar or worse situations for the past few years.

Yet even in pondering all these realities, they didn't seem to compare to what would have been an *unethical* and *unjust* decision to stay where I was. I was faced with a dilemma. I no longer touched *passion, joy, peace, and freedom*—all the virtues the human spirit longs to embrace and has a right to. I was not fulfilled internally while ignorant of what would transpire externally. It is easier to leave a job with another one waiting for you. It is not so easy to do when you don't know, and can't see, what's next. This is the juncture in one's life when faith and hope have to intervene because without them, your heart grows sick and unbelief awaits you with each rising of the sun.

Now if you talked to family, friends, and colleagues who know me, you might hear them say that I am very optimistic and positive in my approach toward life. I simply believe that as I think, so I am. Therefore, I arise each day conditioning my mind to consider that all things work together on my behalf and that anything perceived negatively will ultimately play to my advantage. That's a good way to live, but since I am not perfect, I don't always cultivate that attitude.

Let's be honest—sometimes we want to dwell in a pit of depression and hope that circumstances and situations magically disappear. I know this from experience. Especially in this season of my life, I had moments of uncertainty, fear, doubt, concern, worry, and deep hurt. It was bigger than employment ending. I saw relationships and my future becoming nonexistent because this shift was so *unexpected*. There was great pain as I expanded my reality to a place where limitations whispered to me every day. I knew I needed the greatest exercise of faith that I had ever experienced in my life because *Isolation* had patiently waited her turn to dance with me in this moment.

Stagnant is being characterized by lack of development, advancement, or progressive movement.

Nonetheless, I accepted the path my life was taking and moved forward to attain the prize set before me. It wasn't easy, but being *stagnant* presented a far more painful outcome. According to Dictionary.com, stagnant is being characterized by lack of development, advancement, or progressive movement.[2] I had no longer enjoyed my career. It was taking time away from my family (important, given how significant the development of children is during their first few years); I faced constant criticism when the organization encountered problems; and I carried unhealthy burdens from unrealistic demand (expectations), imbalance, and insufficient resources (people, process, technology, time, and finances). Most important, it was *stripping my true identity*, which is rooted in the image of Christ. I did not like what my life had become and knew that change was the only option. As Sheryl Sandberg once said, "We cannot change what we are not aware of, and once we are aware, we cannot help but change."[3]

I did not like what my life had become and knew that change was the only option.

In the Bible, God instructs Elijah to get away from his current location and go to a place by the Brook Cherith (reference 1 Kings 17:1–7). By the brook, God provided him with water and commanded ravens to feed him. Now you might be saying, "I wouldn't want a raven feeding

[2] *Dictionary.com*, "Stagnant," accessed May 2013, http://dictionary.reference.com/browse/stagnant?s=t.
[3] *Good Reads*, "Sheryl Sandberg Quotes," accessed May 2013, http://www.goodreads.com/author/quotes/5333595.Sheryl_Sandberg.

me." Be careful. The focus here is not on the instrument of the provision but on the source. Elijah had no issues with the ravens feeding him because he knew the plan was orchestrated by God. There are times God will supply your need, and you may not necessarily agree with how He does it. As long as God is behind it, you are good.

Later, the Bible records that "after a while, the brook dried up because there had been no rain in the land" (1 Kings 17:7). I had come to a realization that for me, the brook by which I was standing had dried up, and it was time to move on. When passion is depleted of the organic nutrients it needs to grow, know that a shift is on your horizon. There you find the need to make a major decision. It is the point when you no longer see the appreciation or fruit of your labor, and you must change your climate to prepare for your next harvest. It is the point in which most people would say they are numb and *going through the motions.*

When passion is depleted of the organic nutrients it needs to grow, know that a shift is on your horizon. There you find the need to make a major decision.

In his book *Necessary Endings*, Dr. Henry Cloud writes, "The tomorrow that you desire and envision may never come to pass if you do not end some things that you are doing today. Whether we like it or not, endings are a part of life. They are woven into the fabric of life itself, both when it goes well and when it doesn't. On the good side of life, for us to ever get to a new level, a new tomorrow, or the next step, something has to end. For there to be anything new, old things always have to end, and we have to let go of them."[4] As heart wrenching as I knew it would be, it was my time to *let go.*

One of my favorite parables in the Bible is when Jesus speaks regarding a barren fig tree. The parable reads:

A man planted a fig tree in his garden and came again and again to see if there was any fruit on it, but he was always disappointed. Finally, he said to his gardener, "I've waited three years, and there hasn't been a single fig! Cut it down. It's just taking up space in the garden (including depleting the soil and intercepting the sun)." The gardener answered, "Sir, give it one more chance. Leave it another year, and I'll give it special attention and plenty of fertilizer. If we get figs next year, fine. If not, then you can cut it down" (Luke 13:6–9 NLT/AMP).

Did you catch that part about *depleting the soil and intercepting the sun?* When something in your life is no

[4] Cloud, *Necessary Endings*, pages xiii and 6.

longer bearing the good fruit it should, it is incompetent in producing more life and has now become that which is taking the soil and light from the new seeds that need to be cultivated.

I watch *Curious George* with my sons, and as I think about this fig tree analogy, I vividly remember a particular episode. A doctor, Dr. Greenbean, was teaching George about *pruning*. Dr. Greenbean was cutting some branches, and George thought he was hurting the tree because he didn't understand what the doctor was doing. As a result, George tried to *reattach* the branches that had been cut from the tree. To alleviate George's concerns, Dr. Greenbean shared that *pruning* is the act of making a *careful cut* that doesn't hurt the tree at all. He then explained that too many branches are bad news as they *block* the sun and *prevent* the fruit from growing.

When something in your life is no longer bearing the good fruit it should, it is incompetent in producing more life and has now become that which is taking the soil and light from the new seeds that need to be cultivated.

How often are we like Curious George? We don't understand the process of *pruning*, which is why we often view the *cutting* as a negative exercise. Furthermore, even when we do muster the strength, courage, and fortitude to *cut*, afterward we may second-guess ourselves and try to *reattach* what was destined to end. It's like trying to force a puzzle piece into a space that does not fit its shape or putting a 1970 BMW engine into a 2013 model. You can't fit old things into the design of your new life. Take charge and recognize that you have the skill and ability to make a careful incision of whatever is *preventing your good fruit from growing*. While you may feel this is hurting you, it is actually benefitting you and others (the branches) connected to you. In other words, *it's all good.*

You can't fit old things into the design of your new life.

Given our willful desire and unhealthy denial, we often allow something that needs to end run well past its expiration date. As long as it is bearing good fruit, life is good. But the moment a famine or drought thwarts production of the good fruit in your life, you may be faced with the *termination of a season* and can choose to live barren or urgently take action to move to the *next phase of harvest* where continued growth, stability, and life are ready to receive you. I knew that while something I had been committed to for nine years was ending, many new things, including the birth of my fourth son, were beginning. This nonprofit organization had contributed a great deal to my personal development, but it could not get me to my next level.

Dr. Henry Cloud says, "Getting to the next level always requires ending something, leaving it behind, and moving on. Growth itself demands that we move on. Without the ability to end things, people stay stuck, never becoming who they are meant to be, never accomplishing all that their talents and abilities should afford them. Endings are not just part of life; they are a requirement for living and thriving, professionally and personally. Being alive requires that we sometimes kill off things in which we were once invested, uproot what we previously nurtured, and tear down what we built for an earlier time."[5] Furthermore, Dr. Mark Chironna states, "The more stuck you are in things that are dead and lifeless, that have outlived their usefulness, the less awake, aware, and alert you are. Wake-up calls come as unexpected gifts to enable you to be surprised by grace, so that in the joy of new discovery, you can be lifted out of a rut that has held you back from accomplishing what you are intended to achieve. The more awake you become, the smoother your transitions."[6]

At this point, I will turn it back over to Nine for him to articulate one of his roles to you.

---

[5] Cloud, *Necessary Endings,* pages 7 and 8.

[6] Dr. Mark Chironna, "Statement on Transition," posted March 5, 2013, www.facebook.com.

"Thank you, partner, for turning it back over to me and allowing the reader to have a glance at a very delicate time of your life." Reader, I believe that my partner has best set the stage for me to give some definition behind a specific role I played in his life in 2012—the role of *FINALITY*.

Finality is the state, quality, or fact of being final; conclusiveness or decisiveness.[7]

First, let me say that this is one of the most challenging roles I play because of the perception of those impacted by it. It is ordinary for most of you to avoid *finality*, endings, and conclusions, especially when they *aren't* planned. Remember earlier how my friend shared he never saw himself leaving the nonprofit organization he had given so much of his resources? He didn't tell you that he was essentially the right-hand man, and it was once the strategic vision of the organization to appoint him as the senior leader. Surely, you can understand how such memories occupied his thoughts during this time. Something he had enjoyed being a part of suddenly seemed to be dissipating. The future he saw now seemed blurred. Take a moment to truly feel the heart of my partner. Have you ever seen something in which your life was greatly invested come to a *swift and abrupt end*? It might have been a personal

---

[7] *Dictionary.com*, "Final," accessed May 2013, http://dictionary.reference.com/browse/final?s=t.

relationship, employment, or business venture. How did you feel? I am sure a host of words could be used to describe this and still not do your heart justice. Finality is never easy, or in the words of a famous R&B song, "it's so hard to say good-bye." Actually, I don't know that song, but I hear my partner singing it, so I believe he has something else to say.

...

"It's so hard to say good-bye to yesterday..."

Oh, hello. You caught me singing. I didn't realize Nine had turned it back over to me but am glad he did. Dictionary.com defines final as pertaining to or coming at the end; ultimate; conclusive or decisive; constituting the end or purpose.[8] As I was saying, ending something can be quite difficult, especially if your mind settles on your present or past instead of *channeling* toward your future. Now thinking about the present or past can also be constructive if you focus on the *restoration* of the good things you feel you have missed. In my case, I missed time with my family, time to dream, time to pursue my *personal* goals, and time to build relationships that may have never surfaced had I not made the right decision—just to name a few. I think Ron Carpenter Jr. put it best when he said, "When you desire something from your past that you desire to be restored in your present, God will command

[8] *Dictionary.com*, "Final," accessed May 2013, http://dictionary.reference.com/browse/final?s=t.

you to step forward into your future. You get what's in your past by God bringing it to you, not you looking back."[9] In essence, I was looking for time, health (not just physical), passion, and a variety of other commodities to be redeemed and returned to me.

Regardless of one's belief system, it cannot be denied that one of the most astonishing events in history was the crucifixion of Jesus. The Bible records that "from the sixth hour until the **NINTH** hour, there was darkness all over the land" (Matt. 27:45; Mark 15:33; Luke 23:44). Isn't there a darkness you feel when something is ending? It is as if you are in an isolated place of ignorance and confusion. Many mistake ignorance for stupidity, but I mean ignorance in the sense of lacking the knowledge and true understanding as to *why* something has concluded. You wonder if it was supposed to end. Was there something you could have done to prevent the end and could it have ended a different way? Many thoughts run through your mind, and it is not hard to believe that rest is difficult to come by. Well, when you reflect on one of your experiences now or when you encounter an ending in some form soon, know that there is *light* in the midst of the darkness. We will later explore the *life* that results from this light.

"And about the **NINTH** hour Jesus cried out with a loud voice, saying, 'Eli, Eli, lama sabachthani?' that is, 'My God, My God, why have You forsaken Me?'" (Matt. 27:46).

---

[9] Ron Carpenter, Jr., "Message for Redemption World Outreach Center," speech, Redemption World Outreach Center, January 6, 2013.

"And Jesus cried out again with a loud voice, and yielded up His spirit" (Matt. 27:50). John 19:30 states that Jesus said, "It is finished!" I find this of some coincidence; the *coinciding* of the **NINTH** hour with Jesus' *final submission* to what He was sent to do in one dimension of living (life on earth). These mere words tell us that Jesus understood that while this *finality* was of extreme pain, it was of *great necessity*, which we will talk more about in chapter 6. The focus right now is on *finality* and embracing it with the knowledge that it serves a purpose that may not be visible while you are experiencing the moment.

Bringing finality requires that you not only see the need for something to end, but also that you have a vision of your life beyond the ending. Helen Keller once said, "It is a terrible thing to see and have no vision." Without a vision, you will stifle the greatness within you that is looking for its chance to receive the baton at the next level.

Bringing finality requires that you not only see the need for something to end, but also that you have a vision of your life beyond the ending.

While browsing the Internet one day, I read of a term called *learned helplessness*. Developed by Dr. Martin Seligman, this theory, along with its foundational experiments, began at the University of Pennsylvania in 1967 as an extension of his interest in depression. Seligman found *learned helplessness* is a psychological condition in which a human being or an animal has learned to act or behave helplessly in a particular situation— usually after experiencing some inability to avoid an adverse situation—*even when he or she actually has the power to change its unpleasant or even harmful circumstance.*[10] Put simply, people tend to render themselves *helpless* in situations they have the *power* to alter. As Dr. Henry Cloud writes, these people have more of a "well, I guess we just have to ride it out" mentality, not realizing that their time and energy could be better directed.

When you have become very familiar with someone or something, you may need someone else to help you come to grips with the fact that it is time to let go. In 1996, I accepted a summer internship with a telecommunications company in Research Triangle Park, North Carolina, in the Raleigh-Durham area. Given one of my dearest cousins lived in Raleigh, she allowed me to lodge with her during the summer. I loved it, as I was not only able to save on rent but also lived with one of my family's top culinary artists. I knew I was going to be eating good all summer.

When you have become very familiar with someone or something, you may need someone else to help you come to grips with the fact that it is time to let go.

[10] Dr. Martin Seligman, *Helplessness: On Depression, Development, and Death* (San Francisco: W.H. Freeman, 1992).

During my stay, it was brought to my knowledge that my cousin had been with a certain individual in a relationship for seven years. Since I kept constant communication with my cousin, I already knew this individual from a few family events, but this was the first time I learned about the tenure of their relationship. Well, that's all I needed to know before I soon devised a plan. In retrospect, I agree that I should have kept my business to myself. It was not my business; nonetheless, I am grateful that I did what I did.

After the summer ended, I wrote her male friend a letter. I wasn't disrespectful or rude. I simply made some facts known to him, highlighting that I knew it was one of my cousin's sincerest desires to get married and given that they had been together for seven years, he needed to decide where he wanted to take their relationship. With the love for my cousin as my sole motive, I asked that if he did not have any desires in committing to my cousin on another level that he share that with her so she could possibly move on. Well, long story short, he was a bit upset at my sending the letter, addressed it with my cousin (who actually defended my points in the letter), and the result months later was the *finality* of their relationship (by my cousin's choice). The beautiful thing is, my cousin later connected with a great man whom she married and is happily in love with to this day.

Why? Because my cousin realized her former boyfriend was not going to change his perspective on marriage and neither was she. She was not going to allow a dream of hers vanish at the control of someone else. I was a catalyst to the change, but the *true change* began with a decision I could not make for her. As Dr. Caroline Leaf once said, "Our genes do not dictate our destiny, our choices do.[11] There is an endless array of choices you can make at any one moment, but it is you, with your ability to think, who directs the choosing!"[12] My cousin's *choice* moved her into fulfilling a part of her destiny—marriage.

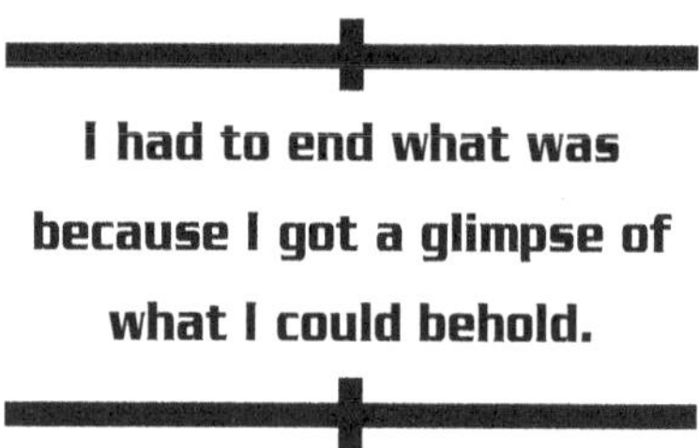

In *Necessary Endings*, Dr. Cloud says we have to "come to grips with the fact that some people—no matter how much you give them or how much you try to help them improve their performance in business or in their personal lives—are not going to change. At least not now and not because of anything you are doing. Accept it, and it will get easier to take the necessary steps to make an ending. You have to be able to let

[11] Dr. Caroline Leaf, "Statement on Choices," posted September 29, 2012, www.facebook.com.

[12] Dr. Caroline Leaf, "Statement on Choices," posted May 8, 2013, www.facebook.com.

go of the very thing, sometimes the very person that the right choice may cause you to lose. You have to see the reality that could be if you would only end what is."[13]

This is what I had to do. When at my *crossroads,* I had to end what was because I got a glimpse of what I could behold. Hmm...*cross*roads. In sharing highlights of Jesus' crucifixion, I believe the runway for the next chapter is now clear. I am going to tackle this one solo; Nine looks forward to speaking to you again in chapter 6.

[13] Cloud, *Necessary Endings,* pages 49, 50, 156 and 178.

CHAPTER 5

WHAT'S UP WITH THAT PLUS (+) SIGN?

Your old lifestyle should not be an option. But as long as it remains an alternate route, you will never be sold out to your new pathway!

—Ron Carpenter, Jr.

Have you ever taken a close look at the construction of the plus sign in a mathematical equation? It looks like a cross with its exquisite vertical and horizontal bars. To me, it is almost as if someone just added the minus sign to the vertical bar and there you have the plus sign. That's probably not how it came to be, but this perspective bears some parallel to your life.

The focus of this symbol is that it *determines the outcome*. Thus far in our story, the plus sign has become associated with the leading number in the equation and it awaits the next number to produce a desired result. I clearly remember the fill-in-the-blank math problems, where you might have the first addend and the answer and have to calculate the missing number to arrive at the answer. For example, 7 + __ = 10. Here, we would fill in the blank with

3. Whatever the number, the plus sign knows its role is to provide an answer *greater* than the individual numbers in the equation. It has the honor and privilege of bringing *gain and increase*. It's what we call synergy—when two things work together to produce a result greater than the sum of their individual effects.

Now what does this have to do with our lives? As we discussed in the previous chapter, *finality* is guaranteed in our lives. It is not negotiable. Every person born into this world will face necessary endings that are challenging to accept yet essential to the progression of their lives. When we reflected on Jesus' death in the previous chapter, we saw how there was darkness over all the land and at about the *ninth* hour, He felt isolated. I cannot even imagine what it was like for Jesus to experience the beatings, mockery, pain, and scorn and then find Himself inquiring whether the Father has forsaken Him. I mean, isn't that how we often feel in the dark *transitions* of our lives? Do you sometimes ask yourself where everyone is now? Where are those friends who frequently smiled with you, hung out with you, dined with you, and ran the minutes up on your phone? Where are those colleagues whom you worked with and joined for happy hour now that this hour doesn't seem

Every person born into this world will face necessary endings that are challenging to accept yet essential to the progression of their lives.

to be so happy? You may even wonder why those family members you could usually depend on for help suddenly seem untouchable. Surely it is agonizing for you to be in such a *pivotal exchange* and feel as if everyone else is numb to where you are. Now, this will make you go crazy, especially if you feel you were there for others at times they felt alone.

Well, this dispensation of solitude can actually work to your advantage. I am not an advocate of living in a silo, void of relationships, but there are moments in your life when you have to silence some voices so you can hear clearly. I can speak to this because I know it all too well. Let me tell you a little about the weekend I made my decision.

On the morning of Sunday, January 15, 2012, my wife, Melanie, came up to me and said, "I know my husband, and I know what you need today. You need time to yourself and with God to ask Him the path He wants us to take. I want to ensure the home is peaceful for you to do that, so I am going to get the boys ready and take them out for a bit." How grateful I was for her to discern what I needed and trust me to hear from God regarding the future of our family. Simply an amazing woman I have!

There are moments in your life when you have to silence some voices so you can hear clearly.

About an hour later, I kissed my wife and sons and said, "I love you. Daddy will see you a bit later." As soon as they left, I rushed upstairs to my closet where I like to have quiet time, set my iPod to shuffle my playlist and postured myself to hear. I knew I needed to hear from God, so I truly had little to say. Often, when we are in a crisis, we want to expend so much time telling God about the crisis and how we are feeling. It's OK to tell Him how you feel, but be careful not to let the problem consume the conversation because given His omniscient nature, He already knows everything anyway. Sometimes praying is saying nothing at all.

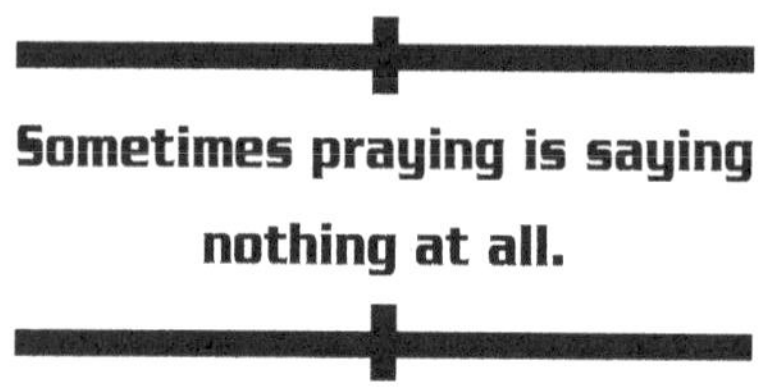

As the music softly played, suddenly tears began to flow down my face. Was I crying because I already heard the answer and didn't agree with it? Was I crying because I just didn't like the reality of my situation? Negative to both. I was crying because, miraculously, every song that *unpredictably* played through my iPod reflected the *love* that God has for me. I knew that God loved me, but it was refreshing in this moment to realize an unimaginable and incomprehensible depth to *His love* that goes beyond any words.

The melodies of love reminded me that God's desire was for me to *live in peace* and to have *life more abundantly* (we will talk about this kind of life later). The lyrics of several songs reminded me that I did not have to live in fear, anxiety, and discomfort. In fact, I still hear the resounding words of one song that said, "The wonder of Your love will break the chains that bind us."[1] Another song built on this message by proclaiming that "nothing can take me from Your great love...I belong to You; I belong to Jesus, no turning back; be set free to know who you are; be set free from the wounds of the past; be set free from the words that have hurt—they weren't true, they weren't true; be set free from the words of the past—do you know that they weren't true, they weren't true, it's not what your Father says over you; be set free from the wounds that won't let you go because the blood of Jesus covers all, it covers all; be set free to know who you are; be set free to know who you are."[2]

I can unashamedly tell you that at this point, my face looked as if someone had just splashed water on it. The tears flowed continually as the resonating theme of *God's love, freedom, peace, and joy* overtook my soul. God was affirming His thoughts of me and sharing the benefits I have through the life He has given me. Why live in a mental bondage when He has *renewed* your mind? Why allow yourself to throw away the notion that you can *daily* experience freedom, peace, and joy? Why believe that your life has to be so unstable that it appears there is a constant struggle? Well, my friend, those are just some of the in-your-face questions we have to ask ourselves when the way we are living doesn't mirror that in which our

[1] Hillsong, *The Wonder of Your Love*, compact disc, (Australia: Hillsong Music, 2010).
[2] Kathryn Scott, *I Belong*, compact disc, (Colorado Springs: Integrity Music, 2007).

Creator designed us to live. *It's the power of choice.* Now I am not suggesting that you live with no boundaries because that wouldn't be God's pattern either. I am simply offering the counsel that you examine every aspect of your life and be willing to make the hard calls where you see misalignment.

As I slowly wiped the tears from my face, God directed me to my answer through a question. His question was, "What did I tell Abram?" (He was later named Abraham.) I knew He had spoken many things to Abraham as recorded in the Bible, but my mind penetrated on one specific reference. In Genesis 12:1–2, the Bible records that "now the Lord had said to Abram: Get out of your country, from your family and from your father's house, to a land that *I will* show you. *I will* make you a great nation; *I will* bless you and make your name great; and you shall be a blessing." The *"I will"* is essentially an if-then statement. IF Abram would first get out of his country, away from his family and from his father's house, THEN God would show him the land, make him a great nation, bless him, make his name great, and make him a blessing.

Well, there it was for me, loud and clear. No room for debate or discussion. It was as plain as *black-and-white*. No gray area. God was telling me to leave the familiar and trust that He had another place set aside for me. My definition of familiarity is when you have adopted a certain way of living to the extent that you resist and reject any level of positive change. There was no need for me to read these lines of Scripture again, hoping for a different context. I now knew the direction I needed to take, and it was soon after confirmed through the *overwhelming peace* I experienced (peace is a byproduct of making the right decision) and a surprise text from a friend (surprise because my friend did not know what was going on with me) who thought of me in that exact moment. My friend's words were accurate to say the least, echoing the *virtues of love, freedom, peace, joy, and faith* that were earlier revealed through the songs. Her encouragement was the final boost I needed to follow through on the decision and allow the next chapter of my life to fully rest in the hands of a Sovereign God whose thoughts and ways are not like ours.

Familiarity is when you have adopted a certain way of living to the extent that you resist and reject any level of positive change.

Having arrived at the destination of an answer, I awaited the return of my family to share with my wife. A couple of hours later, my wife and sons walked through the door, and after getting my boys settled, I told my wife it was time to insert a period and start a new sentence in our life's story. Being the supportive woman that she is, she never once questioned it but merely uttered that she knew we would be OK. In her words, "God's got us." Hearing this further increased my faith and kept doubt away from the six inches in between my ears. So here I was, folks, preparing myself to leave that which had been such a major part of my life to pursue my next path—that which the Lord would show me.

At this juncture, I learned that often God has to release us from the common and familiar business as usual to push us closer to destiny and the fulfillment of His will. And did I mention that He does this by any means necessary? Think of it this way: something you buy in a grocery store is tightly sealed for freshness. My wife recently bought a jar of peaches, and it took all the strength I had to pry that jar open. When finality brings about a tight situation, don't feel constricted by the pain and pressure. Rejoice in knowing that they were only instruments to preserve you and keep you fresh. As those peaches were good to my family and me, so your life will be opened up to *impart goodness* into the lives of others. You were not meant to sit on a shelf. Someone needs to feed off the life you have, but it will rest in the *quality decisions* you make.

When finality brings about a tight situation, don't feel constricted by the pain and pressure. Rejoice in knowing that they were only instruments to preserve you and keep you fresh.

This talk about a tight situation reminds me about what I read in Dr. Mark Chironna's book, *Stepping Into Greatness.* It further supports this context:

Somewhere between the refining crisis and the opportunity to step into greatness is a place we are asked to enter and experience. It is the "hallway." It is the place between our former somewhere and our future somewhere. What gets us to the door of the hallway is the crisis. Something touches our lives that upsets our status quo—something that we thought would last forever changes in a moment. The doorway to the hallway that leads to greatness is opened by grief. Grief is what permits us to move on. Something we thought would last forever comes to an end. We didn't see it coming, and it came without our permission.

In the hallway, we experience great upheaval because we find ourselves being invited to become true to who God made us to be. The hallway is a tight place, and within its corridors, we are invited to embrace a disorienting process of letting go of what was once familiar. Once we pass through the exit door of our crisis and enter into the hallway of process, God sees to it that the door closes behind us. It becomes difficult to turn back.

When a refining crisis touches our lives and there is an ending to what was once familiar, the first thing we do is to try to take some of the familiar things with us into the process. We also try to turn around and go back through the door from where we just came.

> We are totally in the dark, and we can't see where we are going. We have to grope and feel our ways through the hallway. All sorts of emotions rise up inside us in that dark place—anxiety, dread of the future, low-grade frustration, high-grade anger, sadness, despair, and everything in between. That long, dark, and narrow place looks as if it will destroy us, but it is actually designed to build us. What appears to diminish us is actually the tool of God to increase us.
>
> God has arranged it so that there are certain things He allows us to "lose" in the hallway. There are things that we once had a grasp of but don't any longer.[3]

Don't settle for what you see when it's time to move into what you don't see. Or to put it another way, don't be complacent where you are because you have yet to see the full portrait of where you are going. Embrace finality and explore the adventure of branching into something new. Know that it is natural to delve into the agony of *finality*, and it is OK to allow

Don't be complacent where you are because you have yet to see the full portrait of where you are going. Embrace finality and explore the adventure of branching into something new.

[3] Chironna, *Stepping Into Greatness*, pages 91, 92, 94-96, and 141.

yourself time to *grieve*. Grief is a vital component to the healing you *must* have to thrive at the next level.

Have you ever heard a person say, "I just need to get a good cry out" or "I just need one good scream"? I can tell you by personal experience that *a cry or shout does something powerful*. Prior to his death on the cross, the Bible records that Jesus cried out with a loud voice and yielded up His spirit (Matt. 27:50). The process of yielding in the midst of finality should be prefaced by your act of releasing the former life to possess the new life. The cry or shout is merely an outward show of your inward desire to let go in order to obtain. It is your exhale of past successes and challenges so that you might inhale future visions and realities. So I ask you, is it dark right now? Do you feel isolated? Are you experiencing rejection, pain, misunderstanding, confusion, fear, loss of reputation, or loss of friends? Do you feel you need a good cry or scream? Well, go ahead. *Let it out!* As the sound in a cave (dark place) reverberates off the walls in hope that the frequency will pierce the opening, your sound is the landmark for closing one chapter in your life only to announce the unveiling of the next. It's your personal anthem that breakthrough is here!

Your sound is the landmark for closing one chapter in your life only to announce the unveiling of the next. It's your personal anthem that breakthrough is here!

Did you cry or shout? If so, did it make you feel better? If not, it may be that you are in the company of others and it is not quite convenient now. I do understand and probably should have presented the disclaimer that you will want to be alone as you do this. I mean, who wants to work with a person who releases a shout from his or her desk? Others might actually think you are suspect. In your own isolated moment, do this to *bridge yourself* to the next place. I can't tell you what happens in it. I will leave it up to the medical professionals to educate us on how crying and shouting benefit us mentally, emotionally, and physically. All I can say is that they truly benefited me in my dark zone (hallway).

Even after a good cry and shout, know that the journey to heal and navigate through your *transition* is still not an easy one. However, at some point, the pain no longer hinders but rather gives fuel to a relentless optimism for a *new beginning*. Everything is about perspective. Think about a city that you would love to visit for the first time. I would like to visit Paris, France. Do you think I would be miserable if someone wanted to put me on a plane to Paris free of charge? Of course not. I would be ecstatic, and with great anticipation, I would start packing for my trip.

Accept your ending—by building momentum, excitement, and action around where you are going. Your future is waiting for you. Pack your bags and get moving!

Well, that is how you accept your ending—by building momentum, excitement, and action around where you are going. Your future is waiting for you. Pack your bags and get moving!

So what does all this have to do with the *plus sign*? Earlier, I talked about how, to me, the plus symbol can be written by merely adding the minus sign to a vertical bar. Someone may also say it is no different than adding a vertical bar to the minus sign. We all get the picture. The point to extract is this: in this *transitional* period of your life, your gain (vertical bar representing increase) in the next phase of living will be determined by what you are willing to subtract (horizontal bar representing decrease) from your previous phase of living. As hard as it was for me, I had to face the reality that some mind-sets, attitudes, habits, behaviors, and even relationships could not go with me to the next place.

Your gain in the next phase of living will be determined by what you are willing to subtract from your previous phase of living.

"But Author, you don't know how much time I invested into that business or relationship, and now you want me to just let it go?" Yep. Simple answer to a not-so-simple process. The reality is that *they*, whatever or whoever *they* are, have served their purposes. I am not suggesting you start from scratch, move to a different land, and completely shut people out of your life. I am simply saying that you must evaluate *what* and *who* will be a *gain* or *subtraction* in this next walk of life. The *former* (gain) are those who will be there when you exit your cave (dark) experience. The *latter* (subtraction) are those who were only there for a *scheduled* time. In either case, your discernment to recognize the difference is integral to your forward success.

As I tried to apply this concept, I admitted myself into what I call a *transitional detoxification* during this pivotal time of my life. Webster.com defines detoxification as the process of removing a poison or ridding the effect of poison.[4] This is most commonly associated with the consumption of some liquid that will flush your bodily system to remove impurities. After making my decision and closing this significant chapter in my life, I found that many of my conversations were not good for my *new beginning*. Often people have the right intentions but easily draw you back to the past when you are trying to advance. Some of the conversations surface around what they wish you had done, while others center on this notion that if they were in your shoes, they would have done the same thing. The latter is easy to say when you aren't actually in the person's shoes.

Sometimes silence is not weakness or avoidance but instead the indicator that words have converted into action.

[4] *Webster.com*, "Detoxification," accessed May 2013, http://www.merriam-webster.com/dictionary/detoxification.

As my process to heal began, I knew I could not subject myself to certain conversations that would either frustrate me because of people's lack of understanding or steer my focus away from *forward motion.* I removed myself from social media relationships, stopped talking to some people so much on the phone, and truly made myself *invisible.* I even changed my cell phone number. Was this to hurt anyone? Of course not. It was to help me heal and build life's next staircase. Sometimes silence is not weakness or avoidance but instead the indicator that words have converted into action.

As tough as it seems, you reach times like this when you have to silence voices in your life to gain clarity, direction, and *employ the power of focus.* Sometimes people can be your number one hindrance to you bringing something to finality. They can make you decelerate or put on the brakes altogether. When this happens, you forfeit control of your life and decisions to them. My wife was primarily the only person I spoke to on a personal level. I had to separate myself from the noise (distractions), knowing that the true relationships I have would still be there when I *broke out of the cocoon.*

Sometimes people can be your number one hindrance to you bringing something to finality.

The grandiose lesson is that where I felt myself retract, I actually watched my life gain. *Without the pain, there could be no gain.* There is a familiar Scripture in the Bible that reads, "For to me, to live is Christ, and to die is gain" (Phil. 1:21). Even in the *finality* of a thing, you are gaining something else. In Dr. Mark Chironna's book, *You Can Let Go Now*, he says, "Human beings resist change more than any species on the planet. When you get to a place where you embrace change as gain and growth, you are becoming who you were meant to be and are well on your way to wholeness and healing."[5]

That's the principle behind addition. You might conclude one relationship, but two or three others could blossom. You might leave one place of employment but be contacted with multiple offers from other companies. You might, as a good friend of mine did, close your own personal business but gain a totally new perspective on life and begin branching into your other dreams. Some of the simplest advice I give to people is this: let your life unfold. In a culture where patience is widely disrespected, it is difficult to embrace that some matters simply will take time. Don't rush this part of your process. *Let it unfold,* for in this lies your catalyst to the next dimension. Next dimension…shall we go there? Please allow me to bring my friend Nine back into the mix so we may all go there together.

"Nine, are you still there?"

[5] Chironna, *You Can Let Go Now*, page 100.

CHAPTER 6

THE SECOND ADDEND: THE LATTER NINE

(9 + 9 EQUALS 9)

↑

The Second Addend: The Latter Nine

When one door closes, another door opens, but we often look so longingly and so regretfully upon the door that closed that we fail to see the one that has opened for us.
—*Helen Keller*

"Nine? Nine? Hello?"

...

"Yes my friend, I am here. I was simply meditating on the interaction you had with the reader in the last chapter. What a fine exchange that further excited me to share about my other role in this chapter."

Reader, I am so glad you are continuing this journey with us. Unfortunately, I don't get as many customers as my other role. Why, you might ask? Because quite often, people go back to what's *familiar* and *ordinary* instead of launching into the *new* that awaits them. Let's be honest;

you like being comfortable. You like having a rhythm each day you arise and not have that rhythm interrupted. But what if it is interrupted? I am sure it would take you some time to adjust, and that's to be expected.

As with any adjustment, it takes time, and in this waiting period, you must train your mind to think the right thoughts in order to speak the proper words of life and encouragement you need. "Partner, did you have something you wanted to add?"

...

"Yes. Thanks, Nine. I don't mean to interrupt, but I have to interject here."

I love the remarkable story in the Bible of how the children of Israel were delivered from an environment of bondage to enter into a promised place. Yet, even in the *reward promised* in this *transition*, the people complained frequently. Isn't it funny how one challenge in your next phase of living easily provokes you to want to go back to your previous lifestyle? One would think they were crazy because it is recorded that they were brought out with silver and gold and none of them were feeble [lacking strength, weak] (Ps. 105:37). Yet they complained to their leader shortly after their exodus, saying, "Oh, that we had died by the hand of the Lord

You must train your mind to think the right thoughts in order to speak the proper words of life and encouragement you need.

in the land of Egypt, when we sat at the pots of meat and when we ate bread to the full! For you have brought us out into this wilderness to kill this whole assembly with hunger" (Exod. 16:3).

How typical it is for us to revert to the *familiar* the moment we encounter challenge in the *new*. When I made the decision to leave the nonprofit sector and reengage the marketplace (for-profit sector), I was initially optimistic, given the skills I was fortunate to build since graduating from college. However, the unemployment rate, negativity of the media, and reality that I had not worked in the for-profit sector for the past six years were hanging over my head every day. Nonetheless, I pushed myself behind my belief that hope and faith *without* action would profit me nothing. I jumped onboard the career websites, created a résumé (I had not revised my résumé in twelve years), and began charting a plan for this new phase of my life.

I began charting a path, and I gave action permission to operate. I recognized that I needed to exert the necessary effort to thrive in this new world. Often, people "wait" for good things to happen to them. How many times have we heard the phrase "good things come to those who wait"? Well, that can be true only if your perspective of "wait" is correct. Waiting doesn't

Waiting doesn't mean the absence of effort. It means the employment of the right effort in anticipation of the proper reward.

mean the absence of effort. It means the employment of the right effort in anticipation of the proper reward. A *wait*er aims to provide excellent service (action) in expectation of a good tip (reward). I remember Ron Carpenter Jr. saying, "To wait is to prepare for ambush. Sometimes we are so spiritual in praying a door open, but when it's opened, we don't pursue it."[1] In similarity, I once heard George Bloomer say, "Not all forces are broken by a prayer. Many forces are broken by an action."[2] In my own words, don't just sit there. *Be productive and do something!*

In reality, the odds seemed stacked against me, and it became even more prevalent from interview to interview. I felt my résumé was good. After all, it should have been, because I invested in professional help to rewrite it. I seemed to have some of the core competencies still sought in the marketplace. Yet, I wasn't getting the responses I thought, from the countless postings of my résumé to the unique versions of cover letters I drafted. Was I silly or even stupid? I left a guaranteed, biweekly direct deposit to enter a realm of not knowing whether there would be a continual flow of resources in my bank account to take care of my family. If only I could change the events of my past—I would surely not be in this position of having so much responsibility riding on my shoulders and being bewildered as to how it would all be handled.

---

[1] Ron Carpenter, Jr., "Message for Redemption World Outreach Center," speech, Redemption World Outreach Center, November 18, 2012.

[2] YouTube.com, "Spiritual Warfare Pt. 3," accessed May 2013, http://www.youtube.com/watch?v=3DKi_Buqdk4.

One weekend, my optimism elevated as I saw the potential for a changing of the guards in my home. I uttered to my wife, "Maybe I should assume full time care of the kids and matters of the home while you go back to work." Now, some of you might be saying, "How dare he put that on his wife who just conceived another child." Well, if you have been in the home with three little ones for the past couple of years, you will understand why my wife, having already demonstrated a level of success in the marketplace, responded with, "Sure, I will look at some options." Let me pause right here to express appreciation to all the homemakers and domestic engineers. You have the most challenging (and most rewarding) role, and undoubtedly deserve top compensation for what you do on a daily basis.

As a successful professional, the idea of returning to the marketplace piqued my wife's interest. While this was not ideal nor what was best for our children, I figured we needed to put all options on the table and begin to work the process of elimination. So my wife and I decided to take a trip to Atlanta where she might have a moment to share her desire to work for her family's business in a path to inherit it. The visit to see family was great, but the opportunity was not available given the rising instability of the economy.

The company, like many others, simply was not in a position to hire additional staff, local or remote. This increased the burden pressed on my shoulders. What was a guy to do? Would I be able to find something I enjoyed doing that would support the needs of my family? Would I need to let my home foreclose? And actually, more than any of these things, my biggest concern was whether I would be able to continue providing a private education to my children while simultaneously setting aside what they would need in the future to live debt-free. Relating to many men across the globe, this was one of those times where it was difficult being a man, but I knew I had to do it.

As we strolled into the next Monday, I continued my search for the next career move and suddenly realized what would be a turning point. Gravity was beginning to work *with* and not *against* me. Remember in the last chapter how I stated you have to assess all relationships and discern their involvement in your next phase? This was key for me. I could write a book solely on the value of relationships from this experience alone. At the cusp of this new week, I began to consider the relationships I had and whom I could contact for much-needed support. I sent my résumé to friends, old colleagues, and even the headmaster at my sons' school. I wouldn't say this was desperation. It was merely activating one of the greatest treasures you could have in your life—*connection with people.*

I received several responses, some immediate and others delayed, from those I contacted. They expressed their commitment to "keep an ear out," and some of them even proposed networking events I should attend to establish new relationships. Because I was looking for some immediate opportunity to land on my doorstep, it's not hard to believe that I faced frequent moments of discouragement and anxiety. In these moments I would ask my wife, "Do you think I will find something?" And with her *unwavering* support as my biggest cheerleader, she would always say, "Yes, I know you will." So I kept going.

One day I decided to post my career profile and update my résumé on a business networking portal. I knew people who were using this tool, but I never did because of how secure I was (or so I thought) in my previous place of employment. As I entered my work history and uploaded my résumé and profile picture, I was inspired to connect with others utilizing this resource. Let's just say the *action* itself was giving me *momentum.* I began searching for previous colleagues simply to see what kinds of things they were currently doing and what career transitions they had experienced. As I did that, I received a call from a friend of mine who was also my manager in the first company I worked for after graduating college. His words were exciting to me to say the least, and these words were, "If you want back in, I can get you back in." Wow! Here was an opportunity for me to reenter the company that I was charting a successful career path (fast track) with prior to my decision to work in the nonprofit industry. Acknowledging that my career there was six years previously, it was good to know I could tap back into the same line of work. Things were beginning to look "on the up and up." And then...

I had a gut feeling that I needed to keep myself open to other potential opportunities. What? Was I crazy? Was this the same man who was saying he had a family to take care of, but he wasn't jumping on the first promising opportunity presented to him? Yes. I wanted to give myself more time to allow other doors to open for me. It is not that the guaranteed position wasn't a good one. It was simply one of those moments where I wasn't fully settled internally. Some people call it the gut check. At such a bold demonstration of my faith, I believed that *favor* would surround me and other doors would open for me. Thus, back to my searching.

One early Thursday morning, I arose from my bed and decided to call a few former colleagues. Knowing it was early and that they were extremely busy individuals, I didn't expect to reach any of them. I left a voicemail for one person in particular; this individual was *coincidentally* the last person I talked to when I left the for-profit sector in 2006. He was now an executive for another consulting organization. To my surprise and excitement, a recruiter from this business phoned me within hours and wanted to schedule a phone interview with me the next day. My calendar was *undoubtedly* clear as we planned our initial conversation. I must say I was greatly impressed with this company, especially its success in a challenging economic period.

After my first phone interview, I shared with my wife that I wanted to work for them. My hopes were high, but I had my moments of wondering how I would match up in the talent pool. Besides, I had not been in the for-profit market the past six years and was definitely not as experienced as others in the industry. Nonetheless, what started as a mere voicemail to a colleague I hadn't spoken to in more than six years evolved into a career opportunity for me five interviews later. I accepted the position and herein saw the vision further *unfold* that a new life was well underway. Regardless of what could have been viewed as inexperience and limitations, the *faithfulness of God* illuminated so powerfully that I could once again sharpen my focus to see a bright future. My era at an organization I once esteemed had ended, but a *new day was dawning*, and I began to celebrate in the joy of embracing this *new life*!

"Nine, can I turn this back over to you? I'm sorry, but I am getting a little emotional here."

...

"No problem, partner. While I am already aware of your story, it gets to me every time."

You see, folks, that's the *power* of my latter role. Whereas I represent *finality* in one thing, I present *life* in a new thing. That's truly the whole focus in the ending of a thing anyway—to get you to launch into the next thing that is designed to thrust you further into your destiny. When one thing ends, something else is born. This is why you can't stop when something ends. You have to face it, identify the purpose behind it, and then fix your eyes on that which is ahead. Simply put, the *death* (not physically) of one thing is the *beginning of life* for the next thing.

When one thing ends, something else is born. This is why you can't stop when something ends. You have to face it, identify the purpose behind it, and then fix your eyes on that which is ahead.

Now you see the diversity of my roles. In one moment, I bring you to a place that can be *painful to endure*, yet even in that same moment, I am leading you to a place that is *pleasurable*—a place where a *higher form of living* awaits you. It too may have its challenges, but they are only present to fortify you. Ahh…if only more people could get to that place. If only they could defeat the negative mindsets, overcome their unbelief, and renounce the familiarity that grips them, then they could behold the new thing. Wait, what's that I hear? "Partner, is that a baby crying? Is everything OK?"

…

"Yes, Nine, that is a baby crying, and all is well."

I have just experienced the birth of my fourth son, and while each birth has been special, I watched this one more carefully as my wife demonstrated her heroism yet again. It's funny we are talking about the *ending* of one thing so that *new life* can begin, as I don't think there is a more vivid image of this than a woman in the labor and delivery process. We have been through this four times, so let me share what I have seen and relate it to what we experience in the natural events of our lives.

It all starts with a contraction, that sharp, quick feeling of *intense pain* that stuns a mother and causes her to stop whatever she is doing. In the *transition* process to the medical center, the contractions continue as they widen the canal for *great reward*. We check into the hospital, and as we settle into the room, my wife immediately inquires about one of woman's best friends: the epidural. Yes, that calming injection of fluid that numbs the pelvic area and minimizes the pain experienced by the woman during the labor process. This is good *but* can also be bad. The woman, maybe not knowingly, exchanges the reduction of pain for a potentially longer labor process. The epidural provides *relief*, but it can also *delay* the body's aggressive determination to continue contracting. Essentially, this numbness to the pain can *extend* the timeline for the mother to see face-to-face the person she has been nurturing.

Whoa! You saw yourself in that didn't you? How often have you tried to numb your pain in *life's transitions* and found that those coping mechanisms, while appeasing in the moment, are inhibiting your goal? I once read a study that involved more than twenty-three North Carolina hospitals and more than ten thousand deliveries. It stated that a patient who is in labor and who has a cervical dilation of four centimeters or more had approximately one in ten chance of needing a C-section. However, patients who had an induced labor had approximately one in three chance of needing a C-section. The study was driving the message that women should *let labor happen* when feasible.

What am I trying to say? Am I telling a woman to not have an epidural as she prepares to deliver a child? ABSOLUTELY NOT! I wouldn't dare put myself in a position to be stoned by mothers across the globe. Besides, I am so thankful women endure the labor process because we all know men could not do it (cue: men, clap your hands to honor women everywhere). The point I am driving home is that in any critical transition of your life, where one thing ends and the next begins, there will be pain and pressure. Both are necessary and cannot be avoided. *Let your labor happen.*

In any critical transition of your life, where one thing ends and the next begins, there will be pain and pressure. Both are necessary and cannot be avoided.

I had to deal with the *pressure* of still being a provider in my home. I had to deal with the *pain* of some relationships in which I had greatly invested coming to an abrupt end. I had to deal with the *pain* of feeling by myself and troubled by why others wouldn't take this journey with me. I had to deal with the *pressure* of readjusting to the marketplace. In all this, I had to realize it was not just a journey. *It was MY journey.* I hurt deeply, I cried, I questioned where my life was headed, and I wondered why things couldn't have gone a different path. I sought answers to many problems, and clarity (the why did this happen to me) didn't visit me until months after I had already danced with *finality*. When you experience the pain and pressure of life's transitions, accept them as instruments to bringing you into a more prominent place. Your life is deeply rooted in greatness, so where the pain exists is the evidence that a reward does also.

So, getting back to my wife…she had some relief because of the epidural, but the medical equipment is clearly showing that the contractions are shorter intervals than when she was first admitted. Aside from the medical staff, I am the only one present with her in the room. I am not just considered her husband in this moment. I am her coach and biggest fan at the same time. I am frequently *encouraging* her by saying she is doing great and that I am proud of her. She may not have wanted to hear these words at that moment, but you have to be very selective as to whom you have with you in the delivery room, so *choose wisely*. You want the person(s) who will encourage you and speak words of positive affirmation. We simply wait for the body to run its course, for the moment her cervix is ten centimeters

When you experience the pain and pressure of life's transitions, accept them as instruments to bringing you into a more prominent place. Your life is deeply rooted in greatness, so where the pain exists is the evidence that a reward does also.

dilated, and the doctor can say, "Get ready to push." The preference is that the baby is *head down* for the pushing that will move him into the next dimension. Hmm...*head down*. Let's talk about that for a second.

Most of us are familiar with the phrase "as a man thinks, so is he" (Prov. 23:7). This reveals (beyond medical reasons) the significance of the baby's head position. Your thinking will determine how you enter into and flourish in your next phase of living. Let your mind be *renewed daily* with thoughts of hope and a good future. In *Who Switched Off My Brain?*, Dr. Caroline Leaf states, "What you think about expands and grows, taking on a life of its own. The direction this life takes could be positive or negative; you get to choose. What you choose to think about can foster joy, peace and happiness or the complete opposite."[3]

Raise your thinking above what you view as circumstantial limitations. *Ascend* in your thinking by setting your mind on things that are lovely and of a good report (plan). How you exit one thing is how you will enter the next. *Choose your thoughts carefully* because your *new beginning* depends on how your mind is *trained* for the next dimension. In *The 7 Habits of Highly Effective People*, Stephen Covey highlights the principle that mental creation precedes physical creation:

Your thinking will determine how you enter into and flourish in your next phase of living.

[3] Leaf, *Who Switched Off My Brain?*, page 22.

"All things are created at least twice. First is the mental creation or plan; second is the physical creation or work. Highly effective people clearly see the outcome they want in every area of life before they act."[4] In short, *your new world will first be framed by your thoughts, words, actions, and vision.*

Now back to the labor process. The cervix is dilated, and my wife is *ready to push*. Here we go. With every push, she and the contractions are *teaming up* to birth something wonderful. Did you get that? She and the contractions are *teaming up*. They are co-laboring. This is the convergence of where you begin to bring your reward into reality—at the point in which you no longer fight the pain and pressure but instead participate with them, knowing the beauty of what you are about to behold. She is weary, tired, out of breath, and anticipating that both the *process* is about to end and the *new life* is about to begin. For every push, the promise is closer. "Push! Push! Push!" And after a final thrust, the cry of a newborn child becomes the loudest sound in the room. The remarkable has just

This is the convergence of where you begin to bring your reward into reality—at the point in which you no longer fight the pain and pressure but instead participate with them, knowing the beauty of what you are about to behold.

[4] Covey, *The 7 Habits of Highly Effective People*, page 99.

occurred! The unexplainable has just occurred! The child has just entered a new phase of living!

I am sure most of our focus is on the mother in these moments, as was mine, given I had become a professional pregnancy coach. But there is something invaluable to learn from the child as well. Even at such a young age, *the child has already been introduced to Nine,* whether he knows it or not. How so? The child has just seen a previous way of living completely end and within moments was birthed into a new phase of life. *Finality* has spawned a *new beginning.* He leaves a warm place of comfort (familiarity) within Mommy, yet has the immediate support system of family, doctors, and nurses in this new dimension. While the uncertainty of this new world has begun, it is *impossible* for that child to reenter his mother's body (go back to the past). He is at the point of no return. Tip: let it be *impossible* for you go back to that which is now behind you.

Don't give energy to the pain involved. Streamline your focus to the size of the dream, vision, goal, and reality being birthed.

As part of the routine checks postdelivery, the baby's weight is measured. As with all of my sons, the weight always made us awestruck. First son, AJ, eight pounds, nine ounces; second son, Christian, nine pounds ten ounces; third son, Jason, nine pounds, nine ounces; and fourth son, Justin, ten pounds, two ounces. Now you would understand why my wife is my hero. This was my wife's most intense pregnancy and delivery, and Justin was the biggest son we had. How fitting it is that the *greater the pressure, the bigger the reward.* Don't give energy to the pain involved. Streamline your focus to the size of the dream, vision, goal, and reality being birthed.

The joy is within and in front of you. Do what is needed to persevere so you can rest in your new life.

Where are you in the labor process? Are the contractions a bit mild and spaced out? Or with every moment that passes, are the pain and pressure greatly intensified? Has the pressure overwhelmed you to lose hope? Or has it caused you to enlarge (dilate) the reality of your opportunities? Are you participating with the pain and pressure (contractions), or are you working against them, making for a longer, more arduous delivery process? Are you *ready to push* for the joy of seeing what you have had inside finally come to pass?

The book of Hebrews says this about Jesus: "Who for the joy that was set BEFORE Him endured the cross, despising the shame, and has sat down at the right hand of the throne of God" (Heb. 12:2). The joy is within and in front of you. Do what is needed to persevere so you can rest in your new life. My friend, it's your time! There is no drawing back. Drawing back only causes the others your life is to impact to stumble. Just as the child can't reenter the mother's body, you can't revisit the past, the familiar, the common, or the ordinary. *Your new life is ahead!* In salute of my military friends, "Forward march!"

Now, pay close attention. Let me tell you more about this *new life*.

CHAPTER 7

FULL LIFE AHEAD

I came that they may have and enjoy life, and have it in abundance
(TO THE FULL, UNTIL IT OVERFLOWS).
—JESUS (JOHN 10:10 AMP)

As our time nears an end, I hope that you will live life to the fullest. Check out some of these definitions of *full* from Webster.com[1]:

- Containing as much or as many as is possible or normal
- Having all distinguishing characteristics: enjoying all authorized rights and privileges
- Being at the highest or greatest degree: maximum
- Possessing a rich or pronounced quality

I could expound on each of these, but I will leave that for another time. The focus behind these definitions is to motivate you to honestly assess whether your life reflects the

[1] *Webster.com*, "Full," accessed May 2013, http://www.merriam-webster.com/dictionary/full.

attributes of *fullness*: enjoyment, maximum, richness, and quality. *Full life* doesn't mean filling your life (schedules/calendars) with busy activity, which is so prevalent in today's fast-paced world. Activity doesn't equate to effectiveness. Full life means giving those people who and things that are priority and aligned to your purpose occupancy in your life. There should be no room for anything else, so recognize that it may be time to declutter.

At my birthing into a new dimension, the phrase *Full Life Ahead* arose from the depth of my pain to the newfound joy of my FRESH start. I once received a poster in the mail from Joel Osteen Ministries that described FRESH as:

F	Forgive those who have hurt you	Holding onto the hurts and pains caused by others will limit the new thing God wants to do in your life. Forgive the person(s) who hurt you and move forward. Trust that God will make it up to you.
R	Refuse to look back	Whether something happened twenty years ago or twenty minutes ago, learn to let it go and move on. If you'll let go of the old, God has promised He will bring you a new beginning.
E	Expect God's best today	Expectation is a catalyst for miracles. Declare God's favor over your life and expect to see His goodness today and every day. By faith, declare, "I'm expecting God to do something amazing today."
S	Stay in faith and move forward	Don't let circumstances or negative voices steal your joy. Stay in faith, knowing that God will fulfill His promises to you. Today is a new day! Believe that now and enjoy all that God has in store for you.
H	Hope for tomorrow	When you have hope, obstacles become opportunities and setbacks become comebacks. A fresh start in God begins with hope from His Word.

This essentially drives the message I have been trying to convey to you. As Dr. Henry Cloud says, "You do your part, have faith, and tomorrow will take care of itself. But remember, for the right tomorrow to come, some parts of today may have to come to a necessary ending."[2]

Full life means giving those people who and things that are priority and aligned to your purpose occupancy in your life.

While I will give you some *practical* ways in which to navigate through your 9 + 9 journey in the last chapter, I wanted to first expound on the life you were intended to live.

How did I go about exploring this *full life*? I examined *every* part of my life—my faith, family, relationships, finances, health, occupation—you name it. Nothing was untouched. The resonating feeling was an *urgency* to ensure all of them were aligned to this new phase of living. Joy, peace, and freedom welcomed me into my new land. Favor, strength, healing, and love carried me into a new environment. Hope was restored. Time was redeemed. The moment was so sacred that it was as if all that came before it was nonexistent. It was as if I were revived, made alive again, and resurrected!

Gene Edwards says this about resurrection in his book *Exquisite Agony*: "When Jesus arose from the grave, He never once referred to the events of His crucifixion. Not

[2] Cloud, *Necessary Endings*, page 230.

once. Not even one word. Such is the hallmark of all true resurrections! The past is forever gone! Resurrection is beyond that which is dead. Resurrection is a demarcation. The essence of resurrection is that everything afterward is new and has no connection with events of the past. After the resurrection, all things belong to a new creation where the past has evaporated into nothingness. Resurrection living is higher than the life previously lived! Always."[3]

Furthermore, he says, "When you have been hit by the worst possible circumstances and you rise in victory from out of the ashes, those former circumstances have lost their cutting edge. Their power is broken."[4] To further support this, Frank Viola says in *Finding Organic Church*, "This is the principle of resurrection: it is only by death that new life is produced."[5] My friend, regardless of what process has chosen you, no matter the pressure and pain, when you choose to overcome and rise in victory, full life begins! What does *full life* look like for you? For me, *full life* includes but is not limited to the following:

The moment was so sacred that it was as if all that came before it was nonexistent. It was as if I were revived, made alive again, and resurrected!

[3] Edwards, *Exquisite Agony*, pages 91 and 94.
[4] Edwards, *Exquisite Agony*, pages 99 and 100.
[5] Viola, *Finding Organic Church*, page 183.

- Living in the presence of my Creator (peace, love, freedom) through an intimate relationship with Jesus Christ, where I am safeguarded from fear and anxiety.
- Having consistent time with my wife and four sons, as I am first responsible to them. Sidenote: when I was unemployed during my *transition*, having time with my third son, Jason, was priceless. I believe this is when he became so attached to me.
- Properly utilizing the gifts, talents, skills, abilities, and resources given to me to create my now and my future, as well as to serve, encourage, and give to others.
- Rising from my bed knowing there are no limits to what I can accomplish, and implementing the action required to promote my dreams to reality.
- Eliminating financial burdens and establishing wealth, leaving an inheritance for the generations after me.
- Consistently strengthening all relationships through love and support (authentic community with family and friends).
- Personal and professional coaching and mentoring.
- Developing leaders in business, ministry, and academic settings.
- Laughing and being of good cheer.

- Seeking truth versus the acceptance of humanity. Success is fulfilling the will of God, rather than compromising for the acceptance and validation of people.
- Being healthy and well, physically and emotionally.
- Simply doing what stirs my passion and excitement, such as writing and teaching.
- Proper accountability (wise counsel) for continuous learning and development.
- Exercising the power of choice.

Have I accomplished all these things? No. That is a process in itself. I am striving daily. But my focus is not on my present state. My focus is on what lies *ahead*. The present is merely the vehicle that takes me to my destination. As we shared earlier, the key is *acting while waiting*. That's one of the reasons you are reading this book. It was time for me to put *action* behind a dream that has been in me since I was a teenager. My *decision* to end the former life has given me the momentum to *reinvent myself* for this new life. Often, staying too familiar with people and things opens the door for stagnation because of the force

Regardless of what process has chosen you, no matter the pressure and pain, when you choose to overcome and rise in victory, full life begins!

of codependency. But the moment you get a glimpse of who you are and the truth inside begins to unveil itself, there is no stopping you! You were created to experience full life. It should be all you ever know.

I believe in you. I know without knowing you that *greatness* is embedded within every part of your being. You are special. You were made in uniqueness and fashioned in beauty. The only limits you have are those you set. Problems and circumstances can't touch who you are. Choose life! Choose full life! As my friend and mentor Randall Worley says, *"Do what makes you feel alive!"*

Success is fulfilling the will of God, rather than compromising for the acceptance and validation of people.

I love the Bible verse that says, "Therefore choose life, that both you and your descendants may live" (Deut. 30:19). Those you know, and even those you don't know, are watching you because your choosing of life (*full life*) will impart life into them. Your *victory* stamps *victory* on the lives of so many others trapped and imprisoned within the affairs of this life. You can be truth where there is deception, light where there is darkness, love where there is hate, and justice where there is mistreatment. *And the awesome thing is YOU GET TO*

CHOOSE! As Dr. Caroline Leaf once said, "It's not your ability that makes you great…it's your choices!"[6]

Now I am not encouraging pride and arrogance, but you need to *show and tell your full life*! Why? Because the lives you touch have a higher probability of embracing their *full life* when they see someone who has done it. It's kind of like wondering if you could ever become a millionaire and then you befriend one. People need to see full life demonstrated and then be taught how to live on that level.

Jesus paints a good picture to support my case. After His resurrection, the Bible records, "During the forty days after His crucifixion, He *appeared* to the apostles from time to time, and He *proved* to them in many ways that He was *actually alive*" (Acts 1:3 NLV). *His appearance bore the fruit of His resurrection.* Your appearance will bear the fruit of your resurrection—*your full life.*

In the nonprofit organization, I had several opportunities to teach, both in small and large group settings. Knowing that teaching is a passion of mine, one of my friends said, "You know you are going to miss teaching when you leave." My response to him was, "My life will teach." I had instilled within myself a determination that regardless how difficult the ending,

You were created to experience full life. It should be all you ever know.

[6] Dr. Caroline Leaf, "Statement on Choices," posted March 27, 2013, www.facebook.com.

there was a higher level in the new beginning. Let your full life be a witness to how one can soar when they choose to make quality decisions.

If someone could see me struggle, why shouldn't he or she see me prevail, overcome, and prosper? Stay humbled, and let your light so shine that others will see your good works and glorify your God. Here, Jesus shows us the apex of *full life*—that you, in your new creation/invention, should invest time to teach others that they may partake of the *treasure* you have discovered. Albert Einstein said it like this: "Only a life lived for others is a life worthwhile." Be intentional to impart your life into the lives of others!

People need to see full life demonstrated and then be taught how to live on that level.

The resurrection of Jesus emphasizes the pattern of *full life*. Immediately after the death of Jesus, the Bible records that "the earth quaked and the rocks were split, and the graves were opened. Many bodies of the saints who had fallen asleep were raised, and coming out of the graves after His resurrection, they went into the holy city and appeared to many" (Matt. 27:51–53). Wow! This is what *full life* is about. In your resurrecting moment, you are causing someone else—maybe a spouse, child, friend, coworker, teacher, sibling, stranger—to *rise* from their dormancy, sullen state, oppression, dark situation, or coma! When they see someone persevere and move forward with the right mentality, they have the encouragement and strength they need to *propel*. That's a part of community, love, and honoring one another. Greatness within me is cultivated so that life can be shared with others.

Let your full life be a witness to how one can soar when they choose to make quality decisions.

My friend, I am sure you have faced some insurmountable obstacles in your life, but your best times are still in front of you—no matter your age, gender, financial portfolio, etc. Your place of *finality* may be painful and difficult to accept, but for everything that dies, something of life arises. There is so much more for you—dreams, visions, relationships, businesses, patents, and ideas. Don't stay at the place of *finality* where you dwell on what's happened and why. Don't stay in the place of darkness (*transitional* period, where you question and wonder or even complain about why is this going on and you were better off in your previous state). Begin to *speak life* and declare that *you are able*. Declare that all things are working on your behalf. Declare that there are greater things in store for you and that you will begin to see yourself rising up. Say that to yourself even now: "I WILL RISE UP!"

For everything that dies, something of life arises.

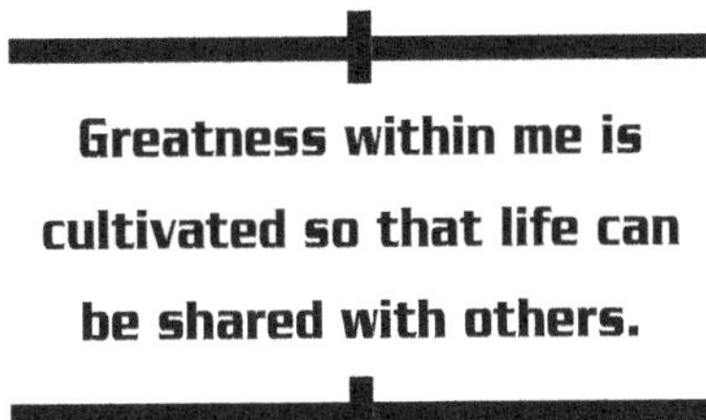

When was the last time you dreamed? Have you ever written your dreams down? When was the last time you set goals for your life and followed plans to accomplish them? When was the last time you took yourself away from all the noise that surrounds you? When was the last time you took care of you, not out of some selfish motive, but out of the desire to impart who you are into others? You are well able to *soar* like the eagle you are. If for no other reason, keep this book with you as a reminder that you have someone cheering you on. *Full life* awaits you, but it's a choice. Will you choose to stay at the place of *finality* or will you choose *life* that many others after you may live? I have chosen *full life*, and I want the same for you. Let's do this together! **FULL LIFE AHEAD... FOCUS ONLY ON THAT WHICH MATTERS MOST!** I will tell you how in chapter 9. But first, Nine has some parting words.

"Nine, please proceed."

CHAPTER 8

9 + 9 EQUALS 9

Events tend to recur in cycles.
—*W. Clement Stone*

It sounds as if my partner will be wrapping up our time together in chapter 9, so I figured I would take this time to say good-bye (*for now*). How fitting it is for this book to have *nine* chapters. Did my partner plan that? Well, I don't know, but it sure was a clever idea if he did.

In this journey, I have learned about you, and you have learned a little more about me than you probably wanted to hear. You probably thought for a moment he was crazy when he told you 9 + 9 was *not* eighteen. Well, how funny it is to end on the same level of *in-sanity* by telling you that *9 + 9 EQUALS 9*. So now you think I am crazy, huh?

Don't get too worked up. I mean, after all that encouragement in the last chapter about a *full life ahead*, we don't need you backstroking. We don't have the time here for me to explore more of the fine roles I play in your life, and that's OK, because once again, that's not the focus. In mathematics, the result is eighteen when I am added to another me. So what's up with 9 + 9 equaling 9? Well let's just add the numbers that make up the answer (18) together (1+8=9). So essentially, 9 + 9 = 18 (1+8, which equals 9). OK, I agree. Don't let your children read this and the first chapter until they are older. We will not be the reason they get the 9 + 9 equation wrong on their tests. Trust me, all this is within good reason. Let me explain and tell you why I am saying good-bye, but only *for now*.

Look at my figure/shape [9]. One of the innate qualities I have is personified by the very top of my figure: *a loop*. Simply put, your life will experience multiple endings and new beginnings. My relationship with you is long term. Let's just say we are in this forever. We are inseparable. The reason I say *9 + 9 EQUALS 9* is because *your life is cyclical*. You will frequently encounter moments of *finality* and *new life*. Don't think that the experiences shared within these pages were my partner's only encounter with me. He has had several and will face many more. But as his friend and mentor Randall Worley told him, his faith is only as good as the object it is fixed on. My partner can share his story knowing that his faith is not in the all-so-common dread of the next *finality* but in the excitement of the next phase of *living* in store for him! In fact, with every necessary ending, he becomes even more confident to handle the next in a diligent pursuit of apprehending the new beginning.

Simply put, your life will experience multiple endings and new beginnings.

The equation of life's transitions is *9 + 9 EQUALS 9*. So while this book is soon ending, it's not a farewell for you and me. It's an ending, yet a beginning, another ending, and another beginning... the role I have in developing you into who you were created to be. So exhale and make the most out of every moment in the journey, and remember, it's not about me or any other numeral friend I know. It's about you and how the events in your life are mere tools for building your purpose, destiny, dreams, legacy, and life! See you around (literally). Good-bye, my friend.

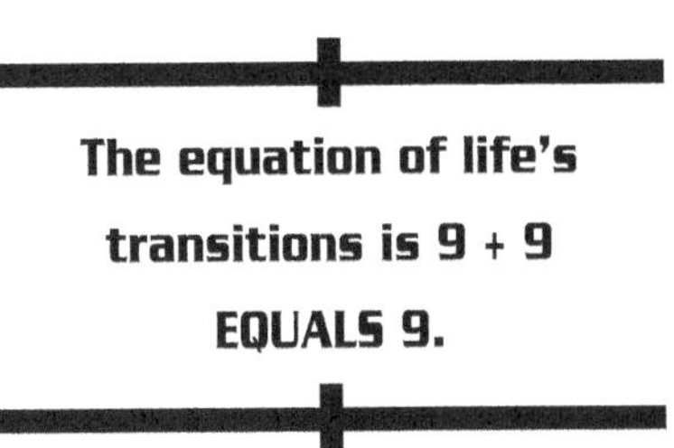

CHAPTER 9

COORDINATES FOR NAVIGATING YOUR 9 + 9 JOURNEY

It is not death that a man should fear, but he should fear never beginning to live.

—Marcus Aurelius

If you are like me, you view inspiration without application as profitless. I would personally consider this work incomplete if it did not include practicality. Thus, I wanted the last chapter of this book to focus on your personal assessment and what you need to do during your 9 + 9 journey. You have heard my story. Now it's your turn. Please allow these principles to be the compass for your 9 + 9 journey. They reflect my personal experience and are references from resources that have strengthened me. I'm cheering you on and already celebrating your new beginning! You can do it!

Disclaimer: *Please do not use this book as a way of escaping/ dismissing a marriage or other provisional family relationship (such as parent to child). If you have major challenges posing a threat to your relationship (i.e., marriage, parenting, sibling, etc.), I would advise you seek professional services to assist you, and where feasible, take the proper measures to protect your relationship.*

See these as principles that make up a dynamic process as opposed to a list of sequential steps.

GET YOUR MIND RIGHT: THINK THE RIGHT THOUGHTS

Philippians 4:8 (NLV) says, "Fix your thoughts on what is true, and honorable, and right, and pure, and lovely, and admirable. Think about things that are excellent and worthy of praise." Dr. Caroline Leaf once said that according to the Word of God *and* science, this is one of the best prescriptions a doctor can write for health.

It all starts with your thinking. When I faced my ending, I had to break toxic thinking and constantly feed myself the right thoughts—the thoughts that God has of and for me.

Jeremiah 29:11 says, "'For I know the thoughts that I think toward you,' says the Lord, 'thoughts of peace and not of evil, to give you a future and a hope.'"

In *Who Switched Off My Brain?,* Dr. Caroline Leaf states we can build a whole new thought pattern within twenty-one days (reference her book for additional details).[1] *Intentionally* train your mind to focus on the right things. To help you, type some positive declarations in a bold, large font and print them on bright paper. Here are a few declarations to consider, just to give you an idea:

- **NOTHING I FACE WILL BE TOO MUCH FOR ME.**
- **GOD HAS A GREAT PLAN FOR MY LIFE, AND HE IS DIRECTING EVERY STEP.**
- **ALL THINGS ARE WORKING TOGETHER FOR MY GOOD.**
- **THERE ARE NO LIMITATIONS IN MY LIFE. GOD IS TAKING ME OVER THE TOP!**
- **FEAR HAS NO PLACE IN MY LIFE. I HAVE POWER, LOVE, AND A SOUND MIND!**
- **I AM FILLED WITH GOD'S PEACE, JOY, AND RIGHTEOUSNESS.**

---

[1] Leaf, *Who Switched Off My Brain?*, page 80.

- **I AM LIVING IN THE BLISS OF GOD.**
- **I WAS MADE TO HAVE *FULL LIFE* AND NOTHING WILL STOP IT!**

**Recommended Resource for Declarations: I Declare, a book by Joel Osteen.*

Post your declarations in spaces you frequent every day—bedroom, closet, bathroom, kitchen, car, etc. As you read them daily, they will help channel *positive energy* to your mental structure.

In the tale *A Little Engine that Could,* a long train must be pulled over a high mountain. Larger engines are asked to pull the train, but for several reasons, they refuse. The request is sent to a small engine, the Little Blue Engine, who accepts the challenge. The engine succeeds in pulling the train over the mountain while repeating, "I think I can." After pulling the train over the mountain, the engine repeats, "I thought I could."[2]

Remember, as a man thinks, so is he. Your thinking will drive your transformation. And the best way to build the right thought life, is to meditate on the Word of God: "Study this Book of Instruction continually.

[2] Watty Piper, *The Little Engine That Could* (New York: Platt & Munk, 2012).

Meditate on it day and night, so you will be sure to obey everything written in it. Only then will you prosper and succeed in all you do" (Josh. 1:8 NLT).

REALITY CHECK: REALIZE THAT SOME THINGS MUST END FOR NEW THINGS TO BEGIN

If you do not first accept that endings are essential, you will never maximize your potential in life. Remember from chapter 5 that *finality is not negotiable*. While I enjoyed my senior moments in high school, college was next for me. While I enjoyed the life of a college student, entry into the marketplace was next for me. Regardless my fulltime status and investment into the nonprofit organization, a change was vital for me. Without these *transitions* and others, my life could have followed a much different path. Allow every experience to grow and develop you but never allow an experience to become your crutch.

Allow every experience to grow and develop you but never allow an experience to become your crutch.

In *Necessary Endings*, Dr. Henry Cloud writes, "The awareness of hopelessness is what finally brings people to the reality of the pruning moment. It is the moment when they wake up, realize that an ending must occur, and finally feel energized to do it. Nothing mobilizes us like a firm dose of reality." Later he adds, "If there is no reason to believe that tomorrow is going to be any different from today, then you finally have gotten to reality. While hope is a great virtue, hope in unreality is not. It is hopeless to continue to do what you are doing, expecting different results."[3]

A key part of your reality check is being able to see the life you want. If you can see it, you can behold it, but seeing it requires you to know that it can only happen once you bring closure to that which keeps it from budding. Be willing to make the delicate cuts to the branches preventing new growth.

INTROSPECT: RECOGNIZE WHAT IN YOUR LIFE NEEDS TO END

"Wisdom is the principal thing; therefore get wisdom. And in all your getting, get understanding. Exalt her, and she will promote you. She will bring you honor, when you embrace her." —Proverbs 4:7–8

Dr. Henry Cloud says, "When truth presents itself, the wise person sees the light, takes it in, and makes adjustments. The fool tries to adjust the truth so he does not have to adjust to it."[4]

---

[3] Cloud, *Necessary Endings*, pages 74 and 89.
[4] Cloud, *Necessary Endings*, pages 127 and 133.

This is where it gets tough, where the rubber meets the road. Webster.com defines introspection as a reflective looking inward: an examination of one's own thoughts and feelings.[5] In the evaluation of your life, you must identify what is a candidate for *finality*. Is it a relationship? Is it a repeated behavior? Is it a business? Is it all the above?

Take this insight from Dr. Henry Cloud in recognizing what needs to end: "The areas of your business and life that require your limited resources—your time, energy, talent, emotions, money—but are not achieving the vision you have for them should be pruned." He further provides some questions to guide your assessment:[6]

- What has the performance been so far?
- Is it good enough?
- Is there anything in place that would make it different?
- If not, am I willing to sign up for more of the same?

These were some of my feelings and experiences confirming the need for *finality*:

---

[5] *Webster.com*, "Introspection," accessed May 2013, http://www.merriam-webster.com/dictionary/introspection.
[6] Cloud, *Necessary Endings*, pages 18 and 96.

- Loss of true identity
- Minimal time with family
- Unrealistic expectations
- Continual anxiety and nervous tension
- Fear
- Contradiction of my beliefs and values
- Lack of encouragement, support, and appreciation
- Blame as a result of the constant criticism
- Having much of my time, schedule, and activities dictated for me
- Lack of productivity
- Restlessness
- Lack of safety and trust
- Frustration
- Struggling to live in joy and peace
- Diminished passion
- Mental and physical exhaustion (fatigue)
- Impediment to other dreams

During introspection, you need to:

1. Make a list of everything that may need to meet *finality*. Don't stumble on whether something needs to be recorded. Start with whatever comes to mind, as you can refine this list later. *Let it unfold.*

2. Next to each item:

    a. Write down your expectations of this candidate. For example, if it is a relationship, write down your expectations of the relationship. Also, it is important to know the other person's expectations of the relationship and how realistically they view your expectations. This should have been done at the beginning of the relationship, but if not, it is a necessity at this point to truly determine if the relationship should end or simply needs to be recalibrated. Thus, a verbal conversation may be needed as part of this assessment.

    b. Write down how this candidate currently makes you feel.

    c. Ask yourself the four questions listed above.

Here's an example to guide you:

Candidate	Expectations	Current Feelings	Evaluation
Friendship with Tim	Share life stories with one another for personal accountability and safety Prayer Partner Hang out and have fun	Frustrated & used; Tim now seems to only call me when he wants something Inequity; no longer feel we are both contributing to the relationship	(Q) What has the performance been so far? (A) Good except for the past 2 years. (Q) Have I made my concerns known? (A) Yes, multiple times, but have seen no improvement. (Q) Is there anything that can make it different? (A) I don't know. (Q) If not, am I willing to sign up for more of the same? (A) No because our friendship is now withdrawing life instead of depositing it.

After executing these steps, you may have an idea of what goes on the chopping block. If that is still unclear, it's OK to give yourself some time to process the information. After all, this is a major decision and turning point in your life. Handle with care. I would go further to say it is OK to share your feelings with others you trust (unbiased relationships). Proverbs 11:14 (NLV) says, "There is safety in having many advisers." However, do not let others determine your decisions. As Joyce Meyer once said, "Hear what others have to say but listen to God."

For any candidates you choose to remove from the list after the assessment, keep them in your hindsight because they came to mind for a reason. Like going to an annual physical with your doctor, set a date in which to measure those candidates to see if they are stagnant or bearing fruit. Recall the parable of the fig tree. You must extend the patience for something to produce good fruit, but when it doesn't, you must extend the willingness to cut it down.

You must extend the patience for something to produce good fruit, but when it doesn't, you must extend the willingness to cut it down.

At the end of the day, be wise in your decisions so that you are promoted to your next season.

<u>**Relational Note**</u>

If your hope is in a person to change, your dependency is in their acknowledgment that change is needed. If you see an issue but they don't, frustration and unfulfilled expectations will continue to be your experience.

OVERCOME PROCRASTINATION: PLAN YOUR ENDING WITH A SENSE OF URGENCY

If you put off what you *know* needs to end, you cannot fully celebrate your *new beginning*. Procrastination should not be an option. The more you delay it, the more likely thoughts of doubt and uncertainty will cause you to second-guess. While closure may be difficult, especially emotionally, don't avoid it with the notion that it will work out in its own timing. See the life you want, and let that drive your urgency to handle anything that could prevent that life from being realized.

See the life you want, and let that drive your urgency to handle anything that could prevent that life from being realized.

In *A Sense of Urgency* by John Kotter, urgency is defined as a "distinctive attitude and gut-level feeling that leads people to grab opportunities and avoid hazards, to make something important happen today, and constantly shed low-priority activities to move faster and smarter, now."[7]

Let's say that after inspecting a vehicle, a mechanic tells the owner he must replace his front brakes immediately. However, the owner decides it can wait. As he is driving one day, he feels himself lose control of his vehicle because his brakes stop functioning. As

[7] Kotter, *A Sense of Urgency*, page 7-9.

a result, he drives into a tree stump. He is OK, but the front end of his car is greatly damaged. What started as a brake problem has suddenly become a much bigger issue. I think you get my point. If you do not exercise urgency and *put the brakes on* something that needs to end, you are stripping your life of the safety it needs to continue growing.

If you do not exercise urgency and put the brakes on something that needs to end, you are stripping your life of the safety it needs to continue growing.

Dr. Henry Cloud says, "What is it that keeps people from throwing things away that they need to get rid of? Usually, it's one of two thoughts: *I might need that* or *I will miss it.* These two thoughts are examples of 'medicating thoughts.' For hoarders, medicating thoughts numb the anxiety that comes from making a decision to part with something they are attached to. They experience anxiety when they hit the moment of truth and know that it is time for an ending, but they get rid of the anxiety by giving themselves a good reason not to act."[8]

For a moment, I told myself I could not end my employment with the nonprofit organization because of my attachment spiritually, physically, psychologically,

[8] Cloud, *Necessary Endings*, page 179.

emotionally, and financially. *It was essentially my life.* How could I thrive without that which had been so significant to me and what I always envisioned was my future? I had to get a broader scope of my life and accept that I needed to give up my current position (with no regret) in order to position myself for the new thing. As a result, I communicated my decision with haste and accelerated my *transition* so I could propel forward.

END IT RIGHT: COMMIT TO BRINGING CLOSURE IN A PROPER MANNER

I recently heard a speaker share that his son ended a relationship by texting. The point emphasized was how technology, while it has its strengths, has contributed to a world where verbal communication is not as popular.

Let me advise you to PLEASE not end any relationship in this manner. Technology is good, but only when used for the right reasons. Be a person of excellence, integrity, and character and treat someone how you would want to be treated. If you struggle in this area, again, get counsel. Plan and schedule the conversation, be kind yet objective based on your assessment (don't let emotions get in the way), speak in love, and never burn a bridge. This does not mean you have to maintain communication or some form of connection with the person afterward. It just means the bridge is not burned through anger, bitterness, resentment, pain, and unforgiveness. At the end of the day, people, whether you know it or not, will be curious as to your "why." But the why is for you. They only need to know that the "how" was executed in love, integrity, respect, honor, and good character. Truth is its own defense.

When people don't have the *truth*, they will surmise "why" you brought closure to something. It's what my friend Randall Worley calls an assumption—the lowest form of knowledge because it has no witness or evidence. At the end of the day, don't focus on what others say or think to the degree it thwarts your power to focus. Remember, your ability to unlock certain doors in your future will be based on how you close those doors now behind you. A slammed door represents chaos. Gently pulling a door closed is the sign of peace, and peace is what you must take with you to your next assignment.

Philippians 3:13 (NLV) says, "Forget the past and look forward to what lies ahead." *Memorialize (bury) the past so the healing can begin.*

Relational Note

If the person chooses to not meet or speak with you regarding the need to end what is, do not let this keep you in bondage. When your attempts have been unsuccessful, plan your own *release* party. Allowing someone else to control your transition diminishes urgency and breeds complacency.

1. Pull out a sheet of paper, and draw a line down the center.
2. On the left side of the line, write your name.
3. On the right side of the line, write the person's name.
4. Take the paper and go stand over a trash receptacle. Then, tear or cut the paper down the middle, asking God to *cut the cord* from the relationship.
5. Embrace the peace you will feel in that moment, and commit to moving forward so your healing can begin.

Allowing someone else to control your transition diminishes urgency and breeds complacency.

Even if the person does meet with you, this is still a good exercise to complete. If what you are ending is not a relationship with someone (such as a behavior you desire to end), you can write that on the right side instead of a person's name.

GRIEVE AND HEAL: TAKE THE TIME NEEDED TO RESTORE YOUR MENTAL, PHYSICAL, AND EMOTIONAL HEALTH

As mentioned in chapter 5, a good way to start your healing process is to release a good cry/shout. There are times my wife will say to me, "I need to get a good cry out." That usually signals to me that she is in a point of *transition* and what's positive is her acknowledgment of how this will help her adjust. This is a part of the internal healing one needs to move forward.

In *Necessary Endings*, Dr. Henry Cloud writes that "the grieving process is a mental and emotional letting go. What that means is to face the reality that it is over, whatever it is, and to feel the feelings involved in facing that reality. It means to come out of the denial and numbness emotionally and feel whatever you feel. When you feel grief, you are saying, I am looking this reality right in the face and dealing with it, the reality that this [whatever this is] is over. Finished. Grief also means I am getting ready for what is next, because I am finishing what is over."[9]

You will do yourself an injustice if you do not give yourself time to grieve and heal. Grieving is not a negative thing. It will help you to move into the next season without anger, bitterness, unforgiveness, or any other negative (toxic) emotion. Forgiving people is not an emotion. It is a decision. Healing *must*

[9] Cloud, *Necessary Endings*, page 213.

involve your forgiving of others. If you do not forgive, you will carry issues in your heart that will resurface, possibly at the pinnacle of your next season. Deal with how you are feeling. Don't push it aside. If you do not forgive, you will forfeit a level of control to that which you just ended.

Forgiving people is not an emotion. It is a decision. Healing must involve your forgiving of others.

When I was in my *transition,* there were days I cried as a form of exhalation. Recognizing the pain I was experiencing was a deep hurt, I registered for a healing class that helped me understand the stones that were building around my heart. I needed to be in a safe place where I could express my innermost feelings. I needed wise counsel, and I needed to vent. While venting is often perceived as negative, it can be very helpful. Dr. Mark Chironna wrote that "there are moments in life when you need to vent. Venting is different from dumping. When you dump, you blame others for where you are. When you vent, you share your feelings in a context with someone who deeply listens to your current emotional state, empathizing with your pressing concerns. Healthy venting enables you to declutter and clear out your heart and mind of psychological debris and spiritual toxic waste."[10]

[10] Dr. Mark Chrionna, "Statement on Venting," posted December 28, 2012, www.facebook.com.

As you recall, I was also able to heal because of my decision to remove myself from certain relationships and conversations during my healing process. I was not being rude. Some conversations were simply not healthy. In the times it hurt the most, only time with God and my family could heal the wounds. When I asked the Lord to help me forgive, His love did a powerful work in me.

Do whatever it takes to heal and know when you have truly healed. It took a friend to honestly tell me I had not healed when I believed the lie that my healing was complete. This is important so that you do not hurt others by projecting your pain onto them. You may have to attend a healing class, invest in some literary resources, find an accountability partner—just commit to yourself that you will not enter your new beginning having not forgiven and released the past. *Let it go and move forward!* While you can't put a timeline on healing, the key is that you put forth the action to facilitate your healing process. In this, be careful not to mistake healing for coping mechanisms (things you might do to make yourself feel better).

Do whatever it takes to heal and know when you have truly healed.

PLAN YOUR FUTURE: PUT ACTION INTO YOUR NEXT PHASE OF LIFE

Having bid farewell to the past, it is now time to lay out the roadmap for your future. I know you believe things will work well, but remember belief *must* be accompanied by action.

During my *transition,* I diligently researched the job market. Having not updated my résumé in twelve years, I partnered with a professional company to rewrite it, and I made it a goal of mine to post my résumé for at least five interested positions on a daily basis. I sent my résumé to personal contacts, and I explored entrepreneurial endeavors. I didn't just "wait" through inactivity. As Ron Carpenter Jr. once said, "To wait is to engage in activity that moves you closer."[11] The key again is to ensure you engage in the *right* activity.

It is tragic to know that many people pass away having never mobilized many of their dreams and ambitions. Be intentional about laying out a strategy for this new dimension. Responses would shock me when I would ask certain friends how they were going to handle an integral part of their lives, and they would reply with "I just have to pray." Now don't get me wrong. I believe in the power of *purposeful* prayer, but I also know that if prayer

[11] Ron Carpenter, Jr., "Message for Redemption World Outreach Center," speech, Redemption World Outreach Center, November 18, 2012.

is not accompanied by action, it in itself can be a crutch or excuse. Could it be that God revealed to you what you need to do but your inactivity is due to your not liking His answer? I will leave that up to you.

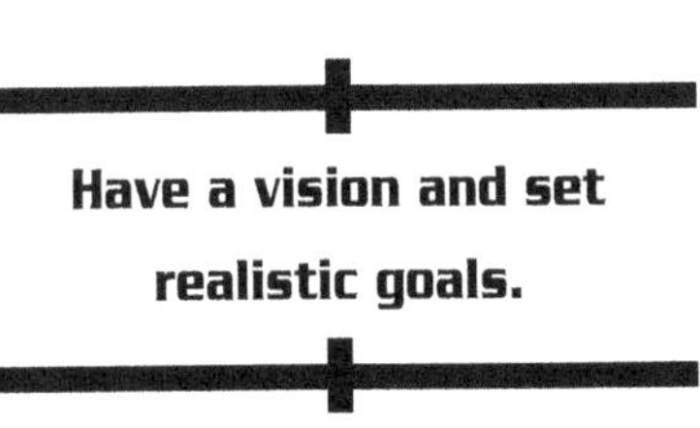

Have a vision and set realistic goals. Proverbs 29:18 (KJV) says, "Where there is no vision, the people perish." In *Courageous Leadership*, Bill Hybels states, "Vision is the energy that creates action. Without vision, people can't focus, can't reach their goals, and can't follow their dreams. Without vision, people lose the vitality that makes them feel alive. Vision is a picture of the future that produces passion."[12]

I am an avid supporter of establishing goals in life. Start short-term: What are you looking to achieve today, this week, or this month? Using my story as an example, let this template guide you in developing your goals:

[12] Hybels, *Courageous Leadership*, pages 31 and 32.

Goal	Become gainfully employed at a company where I can pursue the next phase of my career
Purpose	1. Provide for family. 2. Continual career advancement.
Plan / Strategy	1. Work with professional company to rewrite résumé and cover letter template. 2. Daily post résumé for at least five interested positions via career websites. 3. E-mail résumé to personal contacts. 4. Research tips to prepare for interviews.
Resources Needed	Computer and Internet access
Measurement / Metrics	1. Daily number of posted entries. 2. Job offers. 3. Acceptance of job opportunity.
Timeframe	Four to six weeks.

As you initiate your planning, you might find Bill Hybels' six-by-six framework helpful. The six-by-six concept is facilitated by you identifying six things you must speak energy into during the next six weeks. Keep this list in front of you and frame life around them and all areas of your life by the words you speak.[13] Proverbs 18:21 says, "Death and life are in the power of the tongue." Expect your world to look like that which you are speaking, good or bad.

As you celebrate your short-term milestones, let that momentum reveal a path for long-term goals.

[13] Cloud, *Necessary Endings*, page 115.

ADAPT: RECOGNIZE THAT ADJUSTING TO YOUR NEW LIFE WILL TAKE SOME TIME

Look around. *You are not in Kansas anymore.* You are in a new place. Explore it. Get familiar with your new home. Even plan yourself a New Beginning Launch Party. Put out the welcome mat for yourself and echo words of gratitude in your new residency.

We often live in a world where patience is no longer a respected virtue. When something is wanted, there is the tendency to do what it takes to have it in the moment. Some people call this the microwave age. Do not set the false expectations that you will swiftly adjust to your new life. This can happen but is not the norm. Although I was in the marketplace just six years prior, I still had to reacquaint myself to the environment because of how often things change, not to mention being in a different company.

Expect your world to look like that which you are speaking, good or bad.

When I was seven years old, my dad moved our family from the small town of Winston-Salem, North Carolina, to the major populace of Atlanta, Georgia. I left the comfort of family and childhood friends to migrate to a place where everyone was a stranger. I had to get used to a new school and new teachers, build new friendships, and in the very beginning, live out of a hotel until our home was constructed. As one might suspect, this took some time.

View your *transition* no different from relocating to another city, state, or even country. It will take some time for you to learn the new roads, the landmarks, etc. in this new location. Just as the baby who has to learn how to nurse from his or her mother or take a bottle after being birthed, so you will need to acclimate yourself to your new environment. Be willing to invest in any resources that will aid you in the process.

CONNECT: FORM YOUR RELATIONAL NETWORK

Relationships are one of the most valuable commodities and gifts we have available. Since the beginning of creation, life was formed with the premise that we would relate vertically to a supreme deity and horizontally with one another. Regardless of your relational history, never lose sight of the *power of touch.* If ending a personal relationship caused you great pain and hurt, your trust of others could be diminished. This is why the healing process we talked about earlier is so important. In your new land, you have to avoid both *vulnerability* (connecting with people out of a personal need for acceptance) and *disability* (turning your heart switch off to the cultivation of new relationships).

Examine all existing relationships and open your heart to new seeds. For you to flourish and have the capacity for new relationships, you must properly label any existing ones. Ron Carpenter Jr. once said, "You will not arrive at your destiny by yourself. You must learn and learn quickly who belongs in your life and who doesn't. There are people who need to run with you in your vision. Some people are cemented to you for life (commonly spouse, children, and family), but you will not have many of those. Know who is seasonal and who is lifetime, and don't stir up trouble by putting people in the wrong category."[14]

In *Necessary Endings,* Dr. Henry Cloud says, "Those who are working toward change need people who are committed to their growth. If someone desires change but is still hanging around people who work against that change, the risk is great."[15] People say associations are key. I like to say that *the right associations are key.*

SHARE: TELL YOUR STORY

Did you ever read an autobiography or other book about someone's life story? I am always deeply touched when a person overcomes great odds and adversity in pursuit of purpose. I have friends who have won battles against cancer, and I could never

[14] Ron Carpenter, Jr., "Message for Redemption World Outreach Center," speech, Redemption World Outreach Center, October 14, 2012.
[15] Cloud, *Necessary Endings*, page 106.

grow tired of hearing their stories. Why? Because the power in their testimonies gives me a surge and jolt that boosts me to a higher form of living.

I think what I am trying to convey here is self-explanatory. Your story is a tool to encourage, uplift, and motivate someone else in his or her 9 + 9 journey. You are a pioneer, and those following the path you create need your story to impart life into them. Share your story that others will believe. You have already made a believer out of me.

AN IDEA FOR PARENTS

If you have a child under the age of nine, for his or her ninth birthday, do something special as a rite of passage. You may want to take a trip out of town or plan a ceremony and invite family and friends. Reflect on your child's first years, and then record a vision of what you as a parent anticipate for the next nine years. You may also want key influencers in the child's life (grandparents, teachers, coaches, etc.) to participate. This will take some thought and planning because this is a pivotal *transition*. In the next nine years, your child will be going from the age of nine to a young adult at the age of eighteen, celebrating milestones along the way. Bring finality to the first nine years and set the foundation for your child's future.

If you would like additional information relative to this idea, please contact us via any of the author connect points provided at the end of the book.

REFLECTION

To everything there is a season,
A time for every purpose under heaven:
A time to be born, and a time to die;
A time to plan, and a time to pluck what is planted;
A time to kill, and a time to heal;
A time to break down, and a time to build up;
A time to weep, and a time to laugh;
A time to mourn, and a time to dance;
A time to cast away stones, and a time to gather stones;
A time to embrace, and a time to refrain from embracing;
A time to gain, and a time to lose;
A time to keep, and a time to throw away;
A time to tear, and a time to sew;
A time to keep silence, and a time to speak;
A time to love, and a time to hate;
A time to war, and a time of peace.
—Ecclesiastes 3:1–8

At the close of the day when you close your eyes in sleep, allow the possibility of closure and an awakening to a day where everything has changed.

—Randall Worley

Even all good things end, but only to launch you into the next good thing. At the point something ends, something greater begins. Your life was designed for repeated endings and beginnings. If you can bring closure to what needs to end, you can embrace what needs to begin. Exercise wisdom and rise to the next level.

Full life awaits you, but it is a choice. Your choice.
Do you want it—yes or no?

The opportunity is there.
Will you choose to stay at the place of finality or
Will you choose life that many others after you may live?

**FULL LIFE AHEAD...
FOCUS ONLY ON THAT WHICH
MATTERS MOST!**

NINE THINGS TO PONDER DURING YOUR 9 + 9 JOURNEY

- For everything you have missed, you have gained something else, and for everything you gain, you lose something else. —*Ralph Waldo Emerson*
- Sometimes the best gain is to lose. —*George Herbert*
- He who seeks for gain, must be at some expense. —*Plautus*
- To gain what is worth having, it may be necessary to lose everything else. —*Bernadette Devlin*
- The rewards in life are given to those who are willing to give up the past. —*Robert Anthony*
- I skate to where the puck is going to be, not where it has been. —*Wayne Gretzky*
- Faith is taking the first step even when you don't see the whole staircase. —*Martin Luther King, Jr.*
- Every man dies. Not every man lives. —*William Wallace*
- We must be willing to let go of the life we have planned, so as to have the life that is waiting for us. —*E. M. Forster*

RECOMMENDED BOOKS DURING YOUR 9 + 9 JOURNEY

These are the books I referenced most often while writing this book. I am presenting them for those who may desire to further explore some of the thoughts shared in this book.

Allen, James. *As A Man Thinketh*. New York: Penguin Group, 1902.

Chironna, Dr. Mark. *Stepping Into Greatness*. Lake Mary: Charisma House, 1999.

Chironna, Dr. Mark. *You Can Let Go Now*. Nashville: Thomas Nelson, 2004.

Cloud, Dr. Henry. *Necessary Endings*. New York: Harper Collins, 2010.

Covey, Stephen R. *The 7 Habits of Highly Effective People*. New York: Fireside, 1989.

Edwards, Gene. *Exquisite Agony*. Jacksonville: SeedSowers, 1995.

Hybels, Bill. *Courageous Leadership*. Grand Rapids: Zondervan, 2002.

Kotter, John B. *A Sense of Urgency*. Boston: Harvard Business, 2008.

Leaf, Dr. Caroline. *Who Switched Off My Brain?* Nashville: Thomas Nelson, 2009.

Munroe, Dr. Myles. *The Principles and Power of Vision*. New Kensington: Whitaker House, 2003.

Osteen, Joel. *Become a Better You*. New York: Free Press, 2007.

Osteen, Joel. *I Declare*. New York: FaithWords, 2012.

Osteen, Joel. *Your Best Life Now*. New York: Warner Faith, 2004.

Seligman, Martin. *Helplessness: On Depression, Development, and Death*. San Francisco: W.H. Freeman, 1992.

Viola, Frank. *Finding Organic Church*. Colorado Springs: David C. Cook, 2009.

ABOUT THE AUTHOR

Anthony L. Scott is a grateful husband to his wife, Melanie, and father of four sons, AJ, Christian, Jason and Justin, who lives in the outskirts of Charlotte, North Carolina. He was born in Winston-Salem, North Carolina, but spent most of his life in the Atlanta, Georgia area. He received his Bachelor of Science Degree in Electronics Engineering Technology from North Carolina Agricultural & Technical State University, and has demonstrated professional success as both a management consultant to Fortune 500 clients, and a senior executive in nonprofit operations.

In addition to spending time with his family and friends, Anthony enjoys traveling, playing basketball, reading, writing, and fine dining. Southern-style cooking and Italian cuisines are his favorites, and you would never go wrong providing him sweet tea. He is a leadership coach, personal and professional mentor, minister, and passionate teacher and speaker. Anthony loves to encourage people to overcome their adversities, set and achieve their goals, and cultivate the life they were designed to live.

AUTHOR CONNECT POINTS

Anthony L. Scott would like to personally talk to you and encourage you in your 9 + 9 journey. If you would like to speak to him or have him address your organization in any capacity (staff, team, leaders, students, etc.), please connect with him through any of the channels below.

You may also e-mail us to let us know how this resource has benefited you, and we would appreciate it if you would share it as a source of encouragement for others. We believe everyone who has read this knows of at least one person who is at a crossroads and major transition. Please share the story. Your relational network is our greatest marketing tool. Thank you in advance for your support.

- E-mail: ascott@cite2020.com
- Facebook: facebook.com/cite2020
- Twitter: @cite2020

Made in the USA
Columbia, SC
26 July 2018